Hope Unshakeable

Grandchild Loss

Acknowledgement:

We are extremely grateful to the many people who have helped us put this workbook together.

To the families who so graciously shared their stories in this workbook, thank you for being vulnerable with your loss story.

To the families who walked with us in our pilot small groups, thank you for being brave enough to participate and help make this study what it has become.

To our friends and family who have helped with the editing process, thank you for being honest with us on wording and grammar, as well as the content corrections needed.

To our Hope Family Care families, thank you for giving us the honor of walking with you on your grief journey. You are the reason we are doing this!

To all of the children that are waiting for us in Heaven, thank you for being such a beautiful part of our lives. Because of you, we look forward to Heaven in a new way.

To our Heavenly Father, thank you for giving us our children that are now with You. Thank you for loving us enough to enter into our pain and sit with us, comfort us, and walk with us. Thank you for being willing to experience our pain of child loss. We can know You more intimately because You have walked the road we walk.

Table of Contents

Letter to Grandparents

Dear Grandparents,

First of all, we are so sorry for your loss. We know how much you miss your grandchild and the pain you are going through. You are not alone!

We are confident that there is purpose in each of our stories of pain. No matter how you experienced your loss, or the amount of time that has passed, it is not meaningless. We have found this to be true in our own lives, and in the lives of so many other families that Hope Family Care has had the honor of supporting across the country and internationally, some of these families have shared part of their stories in this workbook.

While many families have great support in the immediate aftermath of their grandchild's death, much of that support fades over the weeks and months that follow. The families are left to figure out their *new normal* on their own. The reality we have discovered is that grief doesn't just go away. Just like the love you have for your grandchild, it will always be a part of your life.

How do we continue to carry the heavy weight of grief and loss? That question is precisely why we wrote this workbook.

When we lost our daughter, Zoe, we knew we needed the comfort and care of our friends who had also lost a child years before. They had gone through the sudden loss of their son and had come out stronger on the other side. They have done a beautiful job, over the years, of keeping their son as a part of their family and incorporating him into their every day. We knew this was what we also wanted.

Over the past few years, God has had us writing, teaching, and sharing about child loss and grief. Through this, we have discovered there are few resources written specifically to aid grieving parents, and even fewer for grandparents.

Grandchild loss is unlike other types of grief, and many grandparents who have lost a grandchild feel overlooked or forgotten in their grief. Our desire and prayer is that *Hope Unshakeable* will provide the space you need to work through your pain and loss.

Today you are taking the next step on the journey of processing your grief and loss, but maybe one day, you will be using what you've learned to help others. We are all on this journey toward Heaven together, just one step ahead or behind.

Jeff and Mackenzie

About this Workbook

Grief is a journey that is not for the faint of heart. It is a journey that no one ever asks to travel, and most are unaware of until they have to walk it. It is a journey that can feel isolating, however, we want you to know that you are not alone!

As you begin working through this study guide, we want you to understand the heart behind it. The questions presented may be difficult and full of emotional triggers. The purpose is to gently walk with you on your grief journey.

There may be questions you do not want to answer, or perhaps you may answer them, but prefer not to share those answers in the group discussion time. We understand those feelings, we have been there. Our goal is that you would feel safe enough to push yourself to do those hard things. Growth doesn't come without pain. We are confident that, as you walk through these questions, you will walk away from this study a stronger person; you will move forward on this journey.

There are no right or wrong answers for this study, but rather the questions will help you reflect on the journey you are already on. Do your best to complete the readings and questions during the week. The reflection questions from the readings will drive the group discussion time.

Each week you will have three different readings:

Story: The story you read each week is from a grandparent who is walking the same road you are on. The focus is not on the type of loss, but rather on what the grandparent has learned, or is learning as he or she walks his or her grief journey.

Soul-Care: The soul care passages are from the Bible and deal with the topic for that week followed by a mini summary or devotional thought. Our prayer is that they would minister to and refresh your soul as you read them.

Self-Care: The self-care readings are helpful insights regarding grief or faith. As you read them, we pray that they would help bring insight to your grief as you walk this journey.

Thank you for giving us the honor of journeying with you. We anticipate that you will finish this study with a fresh perspective on grief, and that you will have a better understanding of how to walk your grief journey in a healthy way.

We also wanted to take the time to share with you a couple of tips about grieving that many families have found helpful. They are meant to help you better walk with your family, both extended and immediate, that has also been impacted by the loss you are grieving.

The first tip is listen and ask questions.

Many times, people try to *fix* grief for someone else. Grief does not need fixing, but instead, it needs a listening ear.

The story of Job in the Bible contains a great example of this. Job's three friends, Eliphaz, Bildad, and Zophar, come and visit with him after several tragedies that God has allowed Satan to inflict on Job, one including the death of his children. At first, the friends do an excellent job of sitting with Job in his mourning. They are present, but they don't speak.

Unfortunately, a little later in the book, we see them sharing with Job their opinions, or rather their thoughts as to why Job is experiencing the suffering he is in. Simply put, they are wrong, which God confirms at the end of the book.

Many times we have seen people try to *fix* a grieving person's sorrow (oftentimes by wanting them to not be sad). It doesn't need fixing, it needs time for processing. That processing needs to happen in a safe place, with safe people who will listen.

The second tip, which is more of a good rule to follow, when walking with grieving people, is called **Circle of Grief / Ring Theory**. *(While there are variations and names to this theory, at Hope Family Care, we use the term* **Grief Circles** *which we have borrowed and adapted from and article Deann Ware, Ph.D wrote for DailyShoring.com.)*

The basic idea of Grief Circles is that the people most affected by the tragedy (at the center of the circle) have permission to *dump out* or *grieve out* to people in the outer rings of the circle. The people in the next ring can *dump out* or *grieve out* to those in the circles that are outside of theirs, but must *comfort in* or *support in* to those at the center of the circle. As each circle expands, people *grieve out* and *comfort in*.

See the illustration below for child loss.

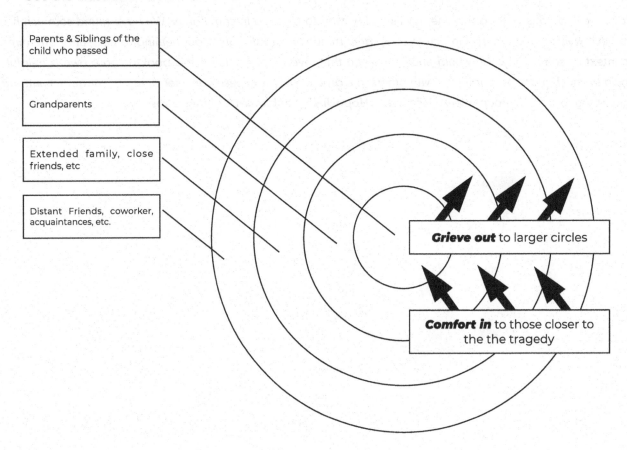

Parents & Siblings of the child who passed

Grandparents

Extended family, close friends, etc

Distant Friends, coworker, acquaintances, etc.

Grieve out to larger circles

Comfort in to those closer to the the tragedy

The idea is that as you encounter someone who is grieving who is closer to the tragedy, you comfort them and then share your grief outward with those further away from the tragedy. This allows for those that are closer to the tragedy to not have to carry the grief of others in addition to their own grief.

Understand that talking about the child who has passed with his or her parents is not the same thing as grieving on them. However, it is important to understand that talking about one's grief or the pain associated with how much one is missing the child with someone closer to the child is only adds to an already heavy burden.

These two tips have been very helpful to the families that we, at Hope Family Care, have had an honor of walking with. We hope that you will find them helpful as well.

As you share in your group times, remember that everyone in the group is part of an outer circle to your specific loss. They will be able to listen to you share and help comfort you, just as you can listen to them share and comfort them when they share.

We are confident that, as your group begins to open up and share, you will find a safe community of people who are walking the same journey as you are. The details of their loss may be different, but the journey is the same. You do not walk the journey alone!

While you can do this workbook alone, it was was written to be used in community. We have found so much healing as we have walked with others. God created us for community, and designed our healing to be found, oftentimes, in the context of community. We would encourage you that, even though doing this book on your own is helpful, you will gain so much more by journeying with others in a group context. Please consider doing this together with others! To find a local or online group, please visit: **www.HopeUnshakeable.net/onlinegroups**

HOPE

STORY
Angela's Story

On November 20, 2018 at 7 AM, two days before Thanksgiving, I was awakened to the worst call of my life. My daughter, Sarah, was on the line and was crying so hard, she could only get out the words, "He is not breathing, we called 911."

This was not the first-time fear had gripped my heart for Rowen, whom we affectionately called "Bubba". The first time was on May 25, 2016, on the day of his birth, when he was born with the umbilical cord wrapped around his neck. He was resuscitated with a *Code Pink* in the delivery room. The second time was on day three of his life, when he was given a *clean bill of health* and sent home from the hospital. At around midnight that night, we received the same kind of call and rushed to their house to find an ambulance and a firetruck there. Bubba had experienced a seizure and had stopped breathing. He was breathing when we got there, but had to spend seven days in NICU and was diagnosed with epilepsy. After a few months on medication he was otherwise healthy, with only a few developmental delays and no more seizures.

We put so much living into those next two and a half years. I took every opportunity to spend with him since his parents had been on the mission field overseas for the first part of her pregnancy and we believed, that at some point, they would probably go back. I loved him with my whole heart (and still do); he was the delight of my life. Six weeks before he went to heaven, I lost my job and was able to spend lots of extra time with him. I was so discouraged by the loss of my job, but I am so thankful for God's grace in getting to spend that extra time with Bubba.

When I received that phone call, on the morning of November 20, 2018, I was beyond worried, but I had hope because we had been through this before. I hurriedly dressed and raced to get to their house, which was only five minutes away. Being a nurse, I hoped there was some way I could help. All the way there I prayed, "God, please let this baby be okay." I arrived at the house and the front door was left wide open with no ambulance or person in sight. I rushed in to find my daughter and son-in-law in shock, crying and saying, "I can't believe this is happening." The ambulance had just left to take my grandson to the hospital. I still had hope that our Bubba had survived until my son-in-law told me that once in the yard, the first responders had yelled, "DOA." The kids hurriedly got dressed and by the grace of God, I was able to drive them to the hospital.

I was there when the doctor came to tell us there was nothing we could do, he had been gone for hours. My husband arrived a few minutes later and we were all allowed to go to the room and be with my grandson. Still in shock, I took care of details — answering questions and doing everything I could to make sure my daughter was okay. She was about four months pregnant at the time and was experiencing a difficult pregnancy. We spent about four hours at the hospital and, during that time, the hall was lined with people from our church. There were so many people the chapel was opened, and food was provided.

Someone asked, "Where will the kids want to go?" I automatically said, "My house."

STORY

So many people were offering to help; I sent friends to our house ahead of us to get our guest room ready, remove Christmas presents from sight that I had purchased for Bubba, to clean, go to the pharmacy, bring food, etc. At the time, I was in my "nurse" and "mom" mode just doing what needed to be done and not considering my own broken heart. I cried at night in our bedroom with my husband, with our daughter, and when I was alone.

Our kids stayed with us for about five weeks, through the holidays. We just focused on surviving the holidays and those first few months. My energy was focused on making sure that my daughter was okay and that the grandson my daughter was carrying would be born healthy. I cried for 120 days straight after Bubba went to Heaven. Much of my grief was in private because I did not want to burden my daughter with my own grief.

Our precious grandson, Bobby was born healthy six months after his brother went to heaven. My father died a month later and my father-in-law died six months later. It was a season of very heavy grief. I was so devastated from losing Bubba that it was months later before I was able to begin to grieve for my dad and father-in-law.

2 Corinthians 1:8-9 (NLT) summarizes the grief for my grandson:

"We think you ought to know, dear brothers and sisters, about the trouble we went through in the province of Asia. We were crushed and overwhelmed beyond our ability to endure, and we thought we would never live through it. In fact, we expected to die. But as a result, we stopped relying on ourselves and learned to rely only on God who raises the dead. And He did rescue us from mortal danger, and He will rescue us again. We have placed our confidence in Him, and He will continue to rescue us."

The grief of losing my grandson and watching my children grieve has been the deepest pain I have ever known. *Through the Eyes of a Lion*, a book written by Levi Lusko after the death of his daughter, helped me survive through those early months. His book, along with the Bible, were my survival guides.

From early on, I realized that this pain was too costly to be wasted. I knew that I had to be transparent about my pain to point others to Jesus. It's been said that pain is a megaphone. When your *worst* happens, the world takes notice and people want to hear what you have to say. There was a unique window of opportunity during that time when we realized that people were intently listening and watching our lives.

Heaven became so much more real to me after Bubba went there. Knowing that I will see him again gives me so much hope. After asking God *"Why?"* so many times, I have found peace in knowing that there are some things I will not understand until I see Jesus' face. I believe that when I look into His eyes, all my questions will be answered, and it will all make sense, but not until then.

As a grandparent, I realized that in taking care to make sure everyone else in the family was okay,

STORY

but my own healing in grief was delayed. In the past year, I finally realized that I suffer from some PTSD from losing Bubba. God is still healing my heart. Through my own grief, God has given me such a heart for people who are hurting, and I have been able to share my story with others who are hurting. Through the blessing of our second grandson, God is showing me how joy and pain can coexist in the same heart. God continues to teach me that He will not waste anything, not even my grief.

I am so grateful for the 919 days we had Bubba with us here. All of those days were such a gift and my life has been forever changed because of them

I believe that I shall look upon the goodness of the Lord in the land of the living!

Psalm 27:13 (ESV)

STORY

Questions | *Reflections*

How does Angela's story relate to your story? How is it different?

_____

_____

_____

_____

_____

_____

_____

_____

_____

_____

What is something encouraging that you see in her story? How can you use that to help you move forward on your grief journey?

_____

_____

_____

_____

_____

_____

_____

_____

_____

_____

SOUL-CARE

Reflections	Scripture

Reflections

_____
_____
_____
_____
_____
_____
_____
_____
_____
_____
_____
_____
_____
_____
_____
_____
_____
_____
_____
_____
_____
_____

Scripture

7 But we have this treasure in jars of clay, to show that the surpassing power belongs to God and not to us. **8** We are afflicted in every way, but not crushed; perplexed, but not driven to despair; **9** persecuted, but not forsaken; struck down, but not destroyed; **10** always carrying in the body the death of Jesus, so that the life of Jesus may also be manifested in our bodies.

16 So we do not lose heart. Though our outer self is wasting away, our inner self is being renewed day by day. **17** For this light momentary affliction is preparing for us an eternal weight of glory beyond all comparison, **18** as we look not to the things that are seen but to the things that are unseen. For the things that are seen are transient, but the things that are unseen are eternal.

2 Corinthians 4:7-10, 16-18 (ESV)

Soul-Care

Devotional Thought

When we sit down and really think about who we are as individuals, we know we are not always as strong as we may appear, or want to appear. Oftentimes, the pressures of life, the situations we find ourselves in, and the circumstances surrounding us show us that we are fragile vessels, jars of clay. At times, we feel like we are barely able to move forward on a normal day, much less when the stress of life increases.

However, we do not give up. Giving up is not an option for us. We cannot give up because we know we need to press on and move forward. We keep moving forward because we know that, even though we may seem fragile on the outside, the true treasure of who we are comes from what's on the inside.

We walk with Jesus.

He is our hope in the midst of the trials of life. He is the one who enables us to move forward. He is the one who brings life from death. He is the one who brings beauty from ashes. He is the one who brings joy from sorrow. He is our hope.

We focus on him, not on what we see around us. That is the key to our moving forward. We know that the pressures, situations, and circumstances of this life (as hard or trying as they may be) are only temporary. We focus, not on those temporary things, instead we focus on what is lasting. The eternal. We focus on Jesus's death and resurrection. That is where our true hope lies.

Reflections

_____
_____
_____
_____
_____
_____
_____
_____
_____
_____
_____
_____
_____
_____
_____
_____
_____
_____
_____
_____

SOUL-CARE

Reflections

Questions

In what ways have you seen God as your source of power as you walk your grief journey? In what ways have you tried to walk on your own?

Take some time to name the things that you feel are trying to *crush* you. After writing them down, pray through them and ask God to help carry the weight of your grief for you.

What temporary things are you focusing on in your life? What eternal things are you focusing on? What are some areas in your life where you need to shift your focus?

SELF-CARE

It's Not Meaningless
Jeff Rollins

Is all this pain really worth it?

As I write this, I am one week removed from meeting with a family hours after their teenage son was shot. The preliminary investigation seems to indicate that it was an accidental shooting that happened due to the mishandling of a gun that was brought to school. Other headlines of the day include a car accident that took the lives of children, and a teenage girl being charged with murder in the shooting of a high school student, a different shooting from the one mentioned above, allegedly having lured him to where he was killed. These three stories were local headlines, while nationally there is the fear and panic at the outset of COVID-19 was beginning to spread.

It's easy to look at what's going on around us, and begin to wonder "What's the point of all of this?" We see so much evil, so many horrible accidents, and so much deep pain on a daily basis. Is it all without meaning?

The death of a grandchild, especially one of ours, can seem like one of the most meaningless tragedies that could happen in life. We are left wondering, "What is God doing? How could a good God allow this? My grandchild was not supposed to die before me. It's not supposed to be this way."

Even though it may feel meaningless, it's not. Suffering and death are not meaningless.

God never wanted us to have to walk through suffering. That was not God's desire. However, it is the reality of the sinful world we live in. Pain, suffering, and death are present in this world because sin is present; sin brought death.

Knowing that this is the reality we live in, our questions need to shift from those above to, *"What do we do now? What do we do with the reality of sin and death in the world we live in? What do we do with the reality of our own tragedy?"*

These are questions we may not have asked before our grandchild's death. They are, however, questions we need to answer. We need to face these questions and begin the journey of answering them. The answers may not come right away, but as we allow ourselves to engage in them, we will find the answers we need to help us as we walk forward.

A unique challenge when grieving the loss of a grandchild is the added component of double grief. Double grief for grandparents is the added grief of watching their son or daughter grieve the loss of his or her child, in addition to the loss of that child as one's own grandchild. The statement isn't meant to be a qualitative statement on the degree to which a grandparent's grief is felt, but rather to see that there are two griefs that need to be processed.

SELF-CARE

Oftentimes, although not always the case, the grief of seeing your son or daughter grieving seems to take the priority over the grief of a grandchild who has passed. This is not a bad thing, but rather it is a grandparent returning to the role of caregiver, as a parent to a child, that may have been set aside as the son or daughter grew up. While the relationship a between grandchild and grandparent is beautiful and precious, the love for a son or daughter and wanting to help alleviate or fix the pain and suffering of their grief can take the immediate focus in the aftermath of grandchild loss.

In a sense, the pain and suffering that grandparents walk though in grieving the death of a grandchild comes in two forms. Both of these griefs are weighty and important; unfortunately, many grandparents tend to minimize one grief and focus on the other.

Much of the time, this minimization is out of necessity so that they can function as caregiver and *push through* their grief to help their son or daughter. Unfortunately, this minimization can lead to a sense of feeling like the pain and suffering that the grandparent or the parents are going through is unimportant and might be overlooked.

Perhaps you felt that way after your grandchild died, and you stepped into a support role for your son or daughter as they grieved the loss of their child.

Our pain and our suffering is not meaningless. So often people can't or don't want to see this. They don't know what to do with it so they deny its purpose or meaning, or avoid looking for it.

Timothy Keller, pastor of Redeemer Presbyterian Church in New York, in his book *Walking with God Through Pain and Suffering*, stresses the lack of conversation regarding suffering in our society as one of the reasons people view it as meaningless. People do not have a place in society that allows them to talk about pain and suffering. They don't know what to do with those realities because people don't talk about them. Pain and suffering don't fit the framework of the American dream of "life, liberty, and the pursuit of happiness."

Oftentimes, the lack of discussion about pain and suffering leads to feelings of confusion and loneliness because the emotions are so heavy, but are never processed or dealt with.

After the death of a grandchild, feelings and emotions that were not part of day to day life before the death, begin to come to the surface. They are true and natural emotions to our situation. If they are not talked about or processed in a safe place, they can lead to feelings of loneliness and isolation. They also have the potential to damage relationships, and cultivate bitterness and resentment, among other things.

The double grief nature of grandchild loss can also lead to a delayed grief, or even a lack of processing of one grief or the other. Many grandparents can feel that their grief is unimportant because

SELF-CARE

they are comparing it to the grief that their son or daughter is walking through. When one's grief is contrasted with or compared to the grief of another and the focus is on the differences, it can often lead to a person getting stuck on their grief journey.

It is extremely important that grandparents recognize that they have two griefs that they are walking through, and that they need to process *both* of those griefs. Delaying grief, whether intentionally or unintentionally, can be healthy for a time, but must eventually be processed.

Processing the grief is not easy, nor is it something that will be quick, but it is an absolutely worthwhile exercise. That is part of the reason we have a *Hope Unshakeable* resource for grandparents. It is important to see the value in walking through pain and suffering.

You may not be able to feel value in it, but you need to trust that it is not meaningless. *"You can't feel it. Either you see it with the eyes of faith and believe it because the text* [the Bible] *says it, or you lose heart."* is what author and pastor John Piper states in one of his messages.

The key to finding meaning and purpose in pain and suffering is found in verses 17 and 18 of 2 Corinthians 4. Again, the passage states that pain and suffering are *"preparing us...as we look not to the things that are seen, but to the things that are unseen."* (ESV)

When you only see what is happening in your life, or happening to you, your pain and suffering will always seem meaningless. When you look down, you only see what is seen. God isn't limited by what you see (the temporary); He operates in the unseen (the eternal) as much as He does in the seen.

You may not see it, but you can trust God to heal the pain. You may not want to, it may be scary and uncomfortable. You may not like what He's doing, but trusting Him is so important. Perhaps that sounds irrational, but in our human thinking, so is the death of a grandchild.

Piper ends his message, *None of Our Misery is Meaningless* with the following words. I think they are a great encouragement to us as you finish this week's readings.

"Don't look to what is seen. When your mom dies, when your kid dies, when you got cancer at 40, when a car careens onto the sidewalk and takes her out, don't say that this is meaningless. It's not. It's working for you an eternal weight of glory. Therefore — therefore — do not lose heart, but take these truths, all the ones you've heard in every message, and day by day, and focus on them. Preach them to yourself every morning. Get alone with God and preach His Word into your mind until your heart sings with confidence that you are new and cared for."

John Piper is founder and teacher of desiringGod.org and chancellor of Bethlehem College & Seminary. For more than thirty years, he served as pastor of Bethlehem Baptist Church, Minneapolis. He is author of more than fifty books, and his sermons, articles, books, and more are available free of charge at desiringGod.org.

SELF-CARE

Reflections

_____
_____
_____
_____
_____
_____
_____
_____
_____
_____
_____
_____
_____
_____
_____
_____
_____
_____
_____
_____
_____

Questions

Take a few moments and write down the suffering you are walking through right now.

What are the questions you have been asking God since your grandchild died? (Prayerfully ask Him whether or not you should change any of them.)

Think about the double grief aspect of your journey. How did you feel the different griefs when you first experienced the loss of your grandchild?

Self-Care

Questions	*Reflections*

Questions

Have you delayed in processing one or both of your griefs? How can you begin to process those griefs? *(Think of a first step for one or the other, don't try to do both at once.)*

What truths do you know, but perhaps you don't feel right now? Which ones do you need to preach to yourself every morning? *(Like what Piper shares at the end of this week's reading)*

In what ways do you need to get alone with God this week so that you can *"sing with confidence that you are new and cared for"*?

Reflections

_____

_____

_____

_____

_____

_____

_____

_____

_____

_____

_____

_____

_____

_____

_____

_____

_____

_____

_____

_____

FAITH

STORY
VICKI'S STORY

FAITH - belief, firm persuasion, assurance, firm conviction, faithfulness. Faith is confidence in what we hope for and the assurance that the Lord is working, even though we cannot see it. Faith knows that *NO MATTER* what the situation is, in our lives that the Lord is working.

My life has encountered many opportunities for me to question my faith; to come to a *Crisis of Faith*. What do I mean by a *Crisis of Faith*? For me, it is that I am forced to ask the question: *Do I REALLY believe what I have learned in the Bible to be true, or not? Do I trust God only when life is good, or can I say I trust Him in the most difficult times?* In the last thirteen years, my faith has been tested more than in my whole 62 years of life.

In December of 2008, my husband and I were excited, as we anticipated the arrival of our first grand-baby, a girl who would be named Averie. My daughter-in-law had to be on bed rest, because of multiple miscarriages, but other than that the pregnancy went well. It was the Friday before Christmas, when my son Djay called and said his wife Karen was heading to the ER, because she had not felt Averie move in a while. I left lunch and rushed over to the hospital. When I got there, I was soon told that they could not find a heartbeat. They had determined that Averie was gone, and Karen would have to wait until Monday to deliver her stillborn daughter.

At the time I was the Women's Pastor at our church and had been in the ministry for ten years. Over the weekend, as we waited to see our granddaughter, I had many questions for the Lord. Like, why? I have served You faithfully and given so much. Why this? Why me? To which I thought, why not me? My mind was a whirlwind that weekend.

As Monday came, and we held our lifeless granddaughter, we cried and continued to try to understand why. The doctors found no reason at all why Averie would never live in this world? So why? Why were all the dreams I had of being a Grammie now shattered?

I struggled with my faith and the goodness of who God is. Why would He allow this? I may never know why, but over the years leading up to 2017, I found myself deepening my relationship with the Lord. It has been such a process to grow, learn and strive to be more Christ-like. Although I will never be all that God is calling me to be on this side of Heaven, each day I will make the journey to try.

In 2017, the Lord took me again to a crisis of faith. What I would go through would stretch and challenge me in ways I never thought I would have to experience? It would take me to a place in my life where I had to decide, did I really believe this faith I have lived all my life? Did I believe God is good no matter what? Did I believe that God can bring good out of heartache?

He promised that He would bring Hope and a future to the Israelites in Jeremiah 29:11 *"For I know the plans I have for you, declares the Lord, plans for welfare and not for evil, to give you a future and a hope."* Did I believe that meant me too? All these questions I had to ask myself during a time when I truly had to believe everything I had learned about the Lord.

In 2017, my husband Jay survived a heart attack known as the *widow maker*, my mother-in-law coming to live with us, the loss of our two and a half year old granddaughter, the flooding of our home during Hurricane Harvey, and the loss of my husband's job. How much more could we take? All of these

STORY

were hard, with feelings of loss and uncertainty, and all of them challenged our faith, but none like the loss of our sweet granddaughter Sadie Ann Miller.

She was funny, independent, sassy, always joyful, and loved queso (ranch dressing was a close 2nd). On June 26, 2017 our family suffered on a day we will never forget. As I was driving to Bible Study that night my daughter Lindsay called me and the next words out of her mouth will live with me forever. "Mom, I am heading to the hospital, Trent ran over Sadie in the driveway, and I don't know if she's dead or alive." I immediately started praying, "Please Lord no, please don't ask us to live without Sadie!! Please let her live!"

As I got to the hospital, I met Lindsay. Sadie had already been transported by ambulance and was in the ER. As they rushed us to the back, my thoughts were still begging the Lord, "Please, no! Please don't take this sweet girl!" Lindsay immediately went back to be with Trent and Sadie. After what seemed to be forever, the doctor came out and told us that she had not survived. There was too much internal bleeding.

It all started that day when Lindsay had come home from shopping with the kids, Michael (6), Cole (4), and Sadie (2). They all unloaded the truck and went into the house while Trent was hooking up his truck to a trailer that needed to be dumped. Once in the house, Sadie decided to go back out and see her daddy as he was pulling out of the driveway. Sadie ran between the trailer and the truck, and as Trent pulled out of the driveway, she got pinned under the trailer wheel. They called 911 immediately and Lindsay and Trent began CPR. As Lindsay says, *"Jesus met her right there in the driveway and took her home."* Sadie was heading out to see her daddy and met her heavenly Daddy instead.

Family and friends gathered in the ER. Tears flowed, prayers were said, and at the end of the night, the loss that was felt was just unbearable.

As I drove home from the ER that night with Jay, Michael and Cole, I knew I had to make a choice: *Do I believe all the things I know about the Lord to be true or will I be angry and blame him for this horrible accident?* In a moment I knew, I truly did believe that God was good, and that He loved Trent and Lindsay more than I did and He would see us through. I promised the Lord that night that I would never be angry or blame Him for the loss of Sadie, and I chose to lean into Him during that time.

Was it easy? Absolutely not. Everyday brought tears and heartbreak, but I knew of God's goodness and I leaned into that as much as I could. I learned what it meant to have the peace that passes ALL understanding (Phil.4:7) It is a peace that is unexplainable. The world could never understand this peace in a time of heartbreak and sadness, but we had it.

Over the next week, we had so many people praying for us and helping in ways that were so extraordinary. Up until this time I had never felt God more through people than I did then. It was like the Lord knew every detail that we needed and provided above and beyond. It was a real community!

STORY

During this time, I realized that not only did I lose a grandchild, but my daughter lost her child. This was new territory for me. How would I put aside my own grief and help my daughter in hers? What can I do? I felt so unequipped for this journey that lay ahead.

As I look back, I can think of things that I could have done better. I tried to do what I could to help, but instead I should have asked Lindsay "What can I do?" I should have just done what I knew was needed. For example, cleaning or cooking. It's hard to ask for help, especially in the pain. We did a lot of hanging out with Michael and Cole so Lindsay and Trent could have some time to rest or do something they enjoyed like watch a movie.

One thing I know I did right was to talk about Sadie often. We would laugh about how much she loved queso, or the funny things she said that we remembered. Lindsay loved watching videos of Sadie, so we watched them together as a family. We still do. The one thing that I knew I didn't want to do was to hover or smother.

As parents, we want to do everything we can to take away the pain our children are going through, but this was a time I couldn't take it away. I could help ease it, but not take it away. We needed to give them the space they needed to grieve as a couple and as a family. Walking this journey has been hard.

I miss Sadie every day, and I have often wondered why God chose us to walk this path. I have learned that Romans 8:28 is true, *"And we know that for those who love God all things work together for good, for those who are called according to his purpose."*

I have been asked how good things can come out of such heartache. I have seen amazing things. People made decisions to follow Christ at Sadie's celebration of life service and days after. To this day, Trent does not walk around with guilt or self-unforgiveness over the accident (a miracle) and Lindsay has been able to talk to other moms who have also lost their child through the same type of accident or some other tragic loss.

So, my answer to the question: Do I trust God? *The answer is always yes.* I have seen it and I know that God is good. He never said this life would be easy, but He did say he would walk through it with us. Jesus told his disciples, *"I have told you all this so that you may have peace in me. Here on earth you will have many trials and sorrows. But take heart, because I have overcome the world."* (John 16:33 ESV)

My faith has grown in so many ways through these trials and sorrows. When I am discouraged I think back to the times God was faithful, good, and showed up in my time of need. He has NEVER failed to do so. He promised to never leave me and I will continue to believe in the truth of God's Word.

STORY

Life was not finished giving us hard times after these losses. In 2019, my other son, Ty and his wife, Kasey miscarried at 20 weeks. Her name is Ellie Kay. When the pandemic hit my husband lost his job. In August of that year, I started the journey of chemo and radiation for endometrial cancer. (At the time of writing this, I am completely cancer free).

I tell you this, not so you feel sorry for our family, but so that you will choose to believe that God is good, even in the many storms. *HE* is faithful and we can have incredible peace no matter what takes place on this road of life on earth. It is our choice, do we continue to love Him and have faith in Him when we are hurting, or do we turn our back and stiff-arm God. I choose to love Him and trust in His goodness and I pray that you will too. He is with you!

Story

Reflections		Questions

Questions

How does Vicki's story relate to your story? How is it different?

What is something encouraging that you see in Vicki's story? How can you use that to help you move forward on your grief journey?

SOUL-CARE

Scripture

2 Count it all joy, my brothers, when you meet trials of various kinds, **3** for you know that the testing of your faith produces steadfastness. **4** And let steadfastness have its full effect, that you may be perfect and complete, lacking in nothing.

5 If any of you lacks wisdom, let him ask God, who gives generously to all without reproach, and it will be given him. **6** But let him ask in faith, with no doubting, for the one who doubts is like a wave of the sea that is driven and tossed by the wind.

James 1:2-6 (ESV)

Reflections

_____

_____

_____

_____

_____

_____

_____

_____

_____

_____

_____

_____

_____

_____

_____

_____

_____

_____

_____

SOUL-CARE

Reflections

_____

_____

_____

_____

_____

_____

_____

_____

_____

_____

_____

_____

_____

_____

_____

_____

_____

_____

Devotional Thought

We are going to face difficulties in life; we can't avoid them, nor can we control all of the circumstances around us. However, we can choose how we respond to those difficulties.

Interruption or invitation? A difficulty can be an interruption into our lives or it can be an invitation to step out of our comfort zone and grow. We get to choose how we see our circumstances.

We may feel like the difficulties we face will not let us experience joy, but it doesn't have to be that way. Joy is not something that depends on what happens around us. As we struggle through difficult times and move forward, we are not only seeing that our faith is tested, but we are proving that it is growing. We are maturing.

This may sound easy, but it's not. Facing the death of a loved one, especially our grandchild, can be one of the most devastating tragedies we will ever face in our lifetime. However, we can face that situation with joy. Joy can exist in our lives, even if we are in pain or are grieving.

This type of joy is a sign of our maturity. This is the type of joy that God wants for our lives. It's a joy that only can come from Him. It's a joy that is only found in Him. It is true joy.

SOUL-CARE

Questions	Reflections

Questions

How would you characterize your faith? Does it endure in difficult situations? Does it produce joy?

A mature faith doesn't mean you don't have negative feelings about your loss. God understands your loss and knows how you feel. What are some feelings that you feel about your loss that you need to share with God? *(Perhaps you have been trying to deny them or hide them.)* Take the time to write them out and share them with Him aloud.

After you have finished the question above, take a moment and ask God: "What do you want me to know about these feelings?" Write down what you feel like He is telling you.

Reflections

_____

_____

_____

_____

_____

_____

_____

_____

_____

_____

_____

_____

_____

_____

_____

_____

_____

_____

_____

_____

SELF-CARE

What is Faith?
Jeff Rollins

"To have faith is to be sure of the things we hope for, to be certain of the things we cannot see." (Hebrews 11:1 GNT).

When we think of faith we think of either something we have or something we practice. Oftentimes we speak of faith with the idea that we need to 'have faith' or if we 'have enough faith' something will happen. The idea being that faith is a means (or a tool) to an end.

While there is some merit to faith being a tool, it can be confusing to define faith that way or to explain it to someone else by how it is used. It seems to describe how faith is used more than define what faith is. The idea of how faith is used is further expanded upon in the rest of Hebrews 11 as the phrase *"By faith"* is stated over and over to describe the actions of the people in the rest of the chapter, characters that are considered by many to be giants of the faith.

Different translations of the Greek in Hebrews 11:1 give us more insight into what faith is. Phrases like *"reality of what we hope for"* (NIV), *"conviction of things not seen"* (ESV), *"substance of things hoped for"* (NKJV), *"the proof of what is not seen"* (CEV), can help, but again they leave us wanting to know more about faith.

Because it is such an important theme throughout the Bible, faith is something we should be able to understand. As grandparents who have had to say a final goodbye to a grandchildren, understanding faith is extremely important. It is crucial to walking our grief journey in a healthy way.

As we look to define faith, I want us to understand what it isn't before we define what it is.

Despite what some translations say, faith is not a *proof* or *evidence* of something that is not seen. Those types of statements tend to take the idea of faith too far. *Evidence* or *proof* take away the trust that is required for belief to be called faith. If there is proof or evidence, then it lends itself to no longer exercising faith, as there is always that idea of trusting in what is not seen.

Faith is very similar to biblical hope in that it conveys a strong confidence or assurance that what God promises will happen. However, I believe faith takes hope a step further. In a way, faith is the outworking of hope.

So what is a good definition of faith? In his book *"Raising Kingdom Kids"*, Tony Evans defines faith this way: *"Faith is acting like God is telling the truth...an action done in response to God's viewpoint on the matter."*

I love this definition of faith for two reasons. First of all, in his definition, faith is immediately aligned with God. The thought that we believe God is telling the truth is extremely important. Instead of trusting our thoughts or our viewpoints on our circumstances, we choose to trust that God is the one who knows the truth. The latter part of his definition puts us in alignment with God's viewpoint on the matter.

SELF-CARE

In other words, faith takes me out of a dependence on my understanding of my circumstances (which is imperfect and incomplete) and aligns me with God's understanding (which is perfect and complete). In doing so, I choose to exchange my lack of knowledge for the perfect knowledge of God.

Secondly, Evans's definition takes faith and puts it into action, action based on trust in God. It makes faith an action of obedience on trust in God. This action on faith lines up with all of Hebrews 11.

Another way to look at the action part is from the book of James. He talks about faith and works. Works are (or should be) the natural outworking of our faith. They don't help us obtain faith, but rather they show that we have faith.

To paraphrase Evans's definition: *Faith is trusting God and acting upon that relationship of trust.* Trusting God is key. In a way, our entire relationship with Him can be simplified into the question of *Do I trust God?* That topic, however, is for another time.

Evans shares three excellent concepts about faith in his book that are useful for teaching about faith. I have adapted those concepts to speak more directly to our experience as child loss grandparents.

Our Anchor of Faith Must Hold Us Steady in Our Situation

When we look at our situations, we oftentimes look at things through our understanding. It's natural. We are in our situations or they are happening to us, so naturally we would look at them through our understanding. This can be a good thing, depending on how honest we are or how well we can objectively look at a situation, but oftentimes it can hinder our ability to move forward because we get stuck.

Faith requires us to look beyond ourselves. Faith requires us to trust in something beyond ourselves. Most of us know who we are and what we are or are not capable of, therefore if faith is going to be what helps us navigate life or live our lives the way God would have us, it must be attached to an understanding or knowledge that is greater than ourselves.

Evans makes this statement. *"Faith is only as strong as the thing to which it is anchored."* While that may seem like a simple statement, the implications of it are of the utmost importance.

When I was in high school I had the opportunity to go out on a private yacht. It was a beautiful seventy-three foot vessel with multiple bedrooms, a kitchen, living ares, and even two wave runners on the back. It was huge! As we were pulling out, the captain asked me if I wanted to help guide the vessel through the canals behind the owner's home out to the Gulf of Mexico. Yes! It was exciting to be able to pilot that boat (a little nerve racking as well, given that there was only about five feet of clearance on either side). When we got out into the gulf we dropped anchor.

There was a special button that was used to drop the anchor and another to activate the winch to weigh anchor. I don't remember specifically the size of the anchor, but I know that it was much larger

SELF-CARE

the tiny anchor that I would use for a canoe and it was connected to the yacht with a large chain, rather than a rope. The yacht needed that anchoring system because a tiny anchor attached to the boat with nylon cord is not close to being strong enough to hold a seventy-three foot yacht steady, even in the relatively calm waters of the Gulf.

The same goes for our lives. When we experience the tragedy of the death of a grandchild we need our faith to be anchored in a way that it will hold us steadfast. The condition of the waters of our lives can move from relative calm to a violent maelstrom in seconds. If our faith is anchored with a tiny nylon cord, we will detach from our anchor and get tossed about by the waves of pain and grief.

In a way, when life is going smoothly, the tiny anchor (a shallow belief in God) and nylon cord for the canoe of our life is enough. When tragedy hits, the nylon cord no longer suffices. We must be tethered by a strong chain to an immovable anchor in order to survive the storms of tragedy that hit our lives.

We must tether our faith in God by trusting His understanding and not leaning on our own understanding. (Proverbs 3:5) In order to move forward through the trials and sufferings in life, we must have our faith anchored to God and his word.

He knows so much more than we do about our situations. He knows how He is going to bring about redemption in a situation where we feel like we can barely survive, much less see Him working.

Are we going to trust Him? Are we going to trust that He knows what He is doing and act upon that obedience or are we going to trust our understanding?

God is our anchor, our trust of Him is what tethers us to that anchor. How strong is your tether?

Our Faith is Revealed in the Storm

Not many people would argue with the thought that God and His word must be our anchor. In fact, most people who acknowledge a relationship with God would not only agree with that statement, but would state that God is their anchor. However, not everyone who would make that claim has had to test their faith and trust in that anchor.

The storms of life reveal our true faith. Tragedy is a revealer of what is on the inside. The way we walk through tragedy and trial will reveal how strongly we are attached to the anchor.

Evans states that "our faith grows in the dark" and I completely agree with him. That is what James is referring to when he talks about the testing of our faith producing steadfastness eventually resulting in our becoming complete and lacking nothing.

However, the dark not only grows our faith, but it also reveals our faith. Much like the stars are revealed at night in the absence of light (which Evans shares), our faith is also revealed in the dark, the absence of calm and comfort.

The storms of this life are much like the dark that Evans talks about. These storms reveal to us our

SELF-CARE

faith and they can also help strengthen our faith. It is in these storms that we see how strongly, or in some cases how weakly, we are connected to our anchor.

When we face the storms of this life, we must confront the reality of how strongly we are attached to our anchor. For some, it is a confirmation of the presence of a strong connection, for others it is the revelation of a connection that isn't strong enough to hold fast to the anchor that will help us get through this storm.

The storms of tragedy reveal to us what is really going on inside of us in regards to our relationship with God.

The good news is that no matter how tenuous or weak our connection to that anchor, it can be made stronger. I have yet to meet a grandparent whose relationship with God did not change as a result of their grief of losing a grandchild.

For some, the relationship with God grows strained and becomes frayed, sometimes resulting in a temporary or permanent separation. For others, they acknowledge that they need to strengthen that relationship more and run to God. Rarely does it leave that relationship unaffected.

That strengthening of our relationship with God leads us to Evans's third concept regarding faith. That *Faith endures.*

Our Faith Endures

Referring to Hebrews 12, where the author talks about our faith as a race, Evans says the following: "Faith is a marathon. It requires a steady, daily dependence on the character and teachings of God." It is not something that we do once or quickly, but rather it is a continual race or run.

Again, the idea of storms of life help us understand the concept of our faith enduring. Just like the anchor for the yacht that I shared about earlier, I have no doubt that the anchor is strong. *The anchor I used for the canoe is a different story.* The question of our faith shouldn't be will the anchor endure, but rather will I hold fast to that anchor.

Is my relationship with God, wherever it may be, strong enough to endure the storms of this life? To bring it back to the way the author of Hebrews states it, is my faith strong enough to run the race that is set before me? Does my faith have the ability to endure?

This is where we can find the strengthening of our faith in the midst of trials. Just like a runner in a marathon moves forward, step by step, our faith grows through active obedience to God. We move forward when we take the next step.

Elizabeth Elliot, one of my wife's favorite authors, put it this way in her quote of an old English poem. *"Do the next thing."* We need to move forward by doing the next thing. We exercise our faith by doing the next thing. We strengthen our faith by doing the next thing. We grow stronger in our

SELF-CARE

connection to God by doing the next thing He asks us to do.

Faith endures as long as needed. It endures through movement and obedience. It doesn't focus on when it will no longer be needed. It focuses on doing the next thing.

My hope places my faith in God. My faith answers the question, *Do I trust God?* My actions are the evidence that my faith is anchored to God.

Self-Care

Questions

Reflections

Which of the three concepts of faith do you connect with the most? How does that help you as you walk your grief journey?

How has your faith in God changed (good or bad) as a result of grieving the death of your grandchild? Where are you now in your faith with God?

Take the next few minutes and prayerfully ask God the following questions. What is the next thing that You (God) are asking me to do? What do I need to do to obey?

TRUTH

STORY
Diana's Story

Truth is defined as a verified or indisputable fact. As a Christian, I believe that God's word is the source of all truth. That definition is so easy to say, but when a tragedy struck our family, that definition was one that challenged me.

Our family walked through the unexpected and unexplained death of my six year old grandson, Thomas. *I love saying his name. Thomas. Even when it makes me cry - I want to hear his name.* Thomas went from a healthy six year old boy reading stories to his little brother to a six year old boy in a hospital bed without brain activity in less than twenty-four hours.

Thomas and his younger brother, Michael, were staying with my husband and me while our daughter was delivering her third child (Ruthie). Thomas complained of a headache around 8 pm Tuesday night. Then he woke up at midnight with a sick stomach, but slept the rest of the night. The next morning he had a slight fever and didn't feel well.

We took him to the pediatrician at 9:30 am Wednesday morning. She examined him and determined it was probably a virus or maybe the flu. She sent us home with a prescription. Once we were home, Thomas laid on the couch and slept.

At 1:15 pm on Wednesday he began to throw up and didn't respond to my voice. We drove the ten minute ride to Texas Children's Hospital and I carried him into ER. He never woke up. His brain began to swell and within a few hours he had no brain activity. Our daughter had delivered our granddaughter six days earlier. And now she was at Texas Children's mourning her oldest son's unexpected and unimaginable death.

Where was God during this time? If you asked me what was true, I would say from my perspective that God was either absent (maybe on vacation) or didn't care. If what I believe about Him being sovereign and in control over every single thing in the universe is true, then He must be *ABLE* to intervene. And if He is able - why didn't He?

While my daughter and her husband experienced a tangible sense of God's presence, I felt nothing. As I sat in the hospital waiting area, I asked a dear friend who had lost her teenage daughter in a car accident how we would survive this tragedy. And she said words which proved to be true. She said *"the truths of God which you have stored in your heart and mind will sustain you."* Her words were the only thing that gave me hope.

I remember saying to my aching heart *"God is good and all He does is good."* (Psalm 119:68) I would say these words over and over again. Friends still mention how they were surprised I could say these words after Thomas died. Let me clarify - *I did not FEEL this was true.* In fact every feeling and emotion told me otherwise. But I resolved for my mouth to speak those words because I hoped that over time that my heart and emotions would grow to be in agreement with the truths I wanted to believe to be true of God and His word.

STORY

The first year after Thomas' death was spent focusing fully on my daughter and son-in-law and the two surviving children. My days were spent in automatic pilot mode thinking of how I could help them survive. My grief was set aside so I could support and care for my daughter's family.

After the first year passed, I recognized that I had not answered the God questions. I still struggled with how God's goodness and His absolute power could both be true. As I allowed myself to dig deeper into my many questions, I realized some of my beliefs and expectations about God didn't line up with the truth of God's word.

I was angry because Thomas' death seemed unfair. I subconsciously believed if I take children for checkups and give them healthy food and care for them in every way possible that they would be safe from disease and live a long life. Sure there were exceptions - but those were for other people and not my family.

I also believed if I just got Thomas to Texas Children's Hospital that they would have all the answers and fix whatever was wrong with him. I mean - that is one of the best children's hospital in the world - right? I believed if I took him to the doctor and the doctor said it was a virus and he should improve quickly that he would be okay *OR* I would quickly know if he wasn't.

My anger with the medical community revealed this wrong thinking. The doctors are not working in their own strength and training. God is the one who works in and through every human to accomplish his perfect plans.

I hadn't reconciled my questions and doubts with Gods truth. What could I have done differently so that Thomas would still be alive? If I had only done this or that things would be different. Once I accepted and surrendered to the truth that God appoints the day we are born and the day we die I noticed the peace began to return to me. (Job 14:5)

As a believer, this world is not my home. (Phil 3:20) This life is not God's best. (John 16:33) Thomas was enjoying the beauties of heaven and in the presence of Jesus. (2 Cor 5:8) Thomas is free of pain, (Rev 21:4) and I am confident that he wouldn't chose to come back to this earth - even if he could.

God doesn't promise me an easy and pain free life. But He does give me peace in the midst of the pain. So as I have accepted His truth - regardless of whether I understand it or not - I have experienced a peace and trust in God.

SOUL-CARE

Reflections

_____

_____

_____

_____

_____

_____

_____

_____

_____

_____

_____

_____

_____

_____

_____

_____

_____

_____

_____

_____

Questions

How does Diana's story relate to your story? How is it different?

What is something encouraging that you see in Diana's story? How can you use that to help you move forward on your grief journey?

STORY

Scripture

17 The Lord is righteous in all his
        ways
        and kind in all his works.

18 The Lord is near to all who call on
        him,
        to all who call on him in truth.

                    Psalm 145:17-18 (ESV)

Reflections

_____

_____

_____

_____

_____

_____

_____

_____

_____

_____

_____

_____

_____

_____

_____

_____

_____

_____

_____

_____

_____

SOUL-CARE

Reflections

_____
_____
_____
_____
_____
_____
_____
_____
_____
_____
_____
_____
_____
_____
_____
_____
_____
_____
_____

Devotional Thought

God loves us. It sounds simple, and may be a little overdone, but it's true. He loves us. That is truth.

Another truth, however, is that we don't always feel God's love for us. This can be especially true when we find ourselves in circumstances that are difficult, like when we have an argument with someone we love, when we get sick or someone we care for is sick, but especially the death of someone we love, like a grandchild.

Those are times when we don't necessarily feel like God is fair and righteous, nor that His love is wrapped in all His works. A verse like Psalm 145:17 can feel untrue because we don't feel His love in what is going on around us.

That's where faith comes into practice, just like we talked about last chapter. Faith is what we need most in those difficult circumstances.

Practicing our faith and trusting God doesn't necessarily mean that we feel better in our circumstances. It just means that we are choosing to look beyond our circumstances and believe that God is faithful. We choose to trust the truth of scripture, rather than the current emotions we are feeling.

Soul-Care

Devotional Thought

God doesn't mind when we struggle to believe He loves us. In fact, He loves when we come to Him in honesty and truth. When we cry out to God in the midst of our difficult circumstances, and we do it without trying to seem like we're doing ok, He is there.

He will always go to those who cry out to him from a place of truth and humility. He is near because He has a deep love for people who are broken hearted. He wants to be there for us.

Sometimes we don't feel Him because we aren't honest with what we are feeling when we cry out to Him. Sometimes we don't feel him because what we are experiencing is so heavy.

Even in the midst of those times, He is there.

Reflections

_____

_____

_____

_____

_____

_____

_____

_____

_____

_____

_____

_____

_____

_____

_____

_____

_____

_____

_____

SOUL-CARE

Reflections	**Questions**

Questions

In what ways have you seen God being fair and righteous in your grandchild's death? In what ways have you not felt like He has been fair and righteous?

Even though you are walking through the grief of grandchild loss, in what ways have you seen or experienced God's love? Have you felt Him draw close to you? If so, how? If not, what do you wish it would look like for Him to draw close to you?

Take some moments to identify the cries of your heart, call out to God from the pain you are feeling. If it helps, write out some of those cries. Then take some time and listen to what He wants to tell you in the midst of those cries. Write down what you sense Him communicating to you.

Self-Care

Death as a Magnifier
Jeff Rollins

Death is a magnifier.

Death will bring to the surface the brokenness that was present in someone prior to the tragedy that occurred. This is true of every death of a loved one, not just that of a grandchild.

When a family is living their *normal* life, prior to the loss, there are negative dynamics that come into play that stem from differences in upbringing, hurts, wounds, habits, selfishness, personalities, etc. We call these negative dynamics the *brokenness* that we carry around inside of us. When things are normal, we usually have the emotional energy to deal with this brokenness in ourselves and others in a healthy way, or at least in a way that allows our relationships to continue.

Many, if not all, families have dynamics that have some level of unhealthy patterns and roles. Much of this is due to the fact that families are made up of flawed humans with brokenness. The degree to which the dynamics are unhealthy is directly affected by the emotional health of those involved.

When looking at grieving the loss of a grandchild, it is important to recognize that there are going to be some sort of levels of unhealthy dynamics that are a part of relationships in general, even without the stress of the death of a loved one.

The death of a grandchild comes in like a storm that disrupts the normal life that we were living. In doing so, the pain and grief of loss become all consuming. The emotional energy that we typically use to deal with our normal lives shifts from dealing with the brokenness of others, to surviving.

Normal routines like making the bed, showering, and even eating are no longer routine, but rather require active focus and concentration that they didn't before. Some of those routines are abandoned altogether.

The resulting effect is that the brokenness that we readily dealt with in others, or even suppressed in ourselves comes to the surface. In a way, the filters through which we once viewed, processed, and lived life are shattered, revealing what we once were able to keep on the inside.

Oftentimes, when dealing with the extended family, grandparents and their children, especially the parent who lost a child, can revert back to some of the dynamics of family life that were present when growing up. This is not necessarily a bad thing, but rather something to be aware of moving forward.

The reverting back to previous roles of family dynamics can put an added stress on grandparents. You may, as a grandparent, feel an enormous weight to try to *fix* things or to try to help *problem solve*. This is normal, but be careful not put extra stress that is not always needed onto yourself as a grandparent.

SELF-CARE

The loss of these filters can cause strains in relationships that used to not be difficult. It can cause stress in marriages and arguments over things that were once easily dealt with. Death reveals relational issues that were previously present, but, prior to the loss, we had the emotional energy to deal with them or set them aside.

So what do we do with this?

First of all, we need to be ready to extend grace and forgiveness. There may be things that your son/daughter, the parents of the child who passed might, say or do that are insensitive or possibly rude to you, as his/her parent. They may put too much of a burden on you to help or might not want you to be around as much as you would like.

These are all dynamics that come directly from the grief that they are walking through. They may not be processing their grief in a healthy way, or they may be so focused on themselves and the surviving siblings, and they seemingly forget you.

This is where grace and forgiveness are so important. That doesn't mean to say that what is said or done is correct, but in order to walk through your grandparent grief in a healthy way, you need to make sure that you are not focused on the actions of the immediate family that lost the child. Death is magnifying the brokenness in them as much as it is in you.

While the loss of filters to suppress brokenness may seem negative, it can be positive. In a way, the loss of a grandchild allows families to see the issues that they may need to work on that were previously masked because of the ability to spend emotional energy on ways to avoid the issue or temporarily address it without a long-term solution. It may also highlight the positive ways you came together as a family to support each other.

The loss allows for these negative issues to come to the surface, but with a new perspective. The struggles that we had prior to the loss can be viewed in light of what truly is important.

Death magnifies the brokenness in us, but it also opens our eyes to the beauty of what truly matters in life. It allows us to have a fresh perspective on our lives.

It can help us see that it is important to care for ourselves and not just others. Many grandparents who have lost a grandchild will feel the burden to be available to their son/daughter at every waking moment, and sometimes when asleep.

While this is helpful, in the immediate aftermath of the loss, over the course of short-term and long-term grief care, it can be detrimental. There must be good boundaries in place that allow you, as the grandparent to be able to care for yourself.

Self-care is not selfish.

Self-care is a vital part of being healthy for the long-term. The journey of grief, regardless of one's relationship to the loved one who passed, is going to be a lifelong journey. It is more of a marathon than

SELF-CARE

a sprint, however, oftentimes grandparents feel like they are sprinting a marathon.

Take time to slow down. Recharge. Refresh. Get help processing your grief. *It is best to process your grief with someone other than your son/daughter.* This doesn't mean that you don't talk about the child who has passed, but rather that you are not talking about your grief about your grandchild who has passed with the parents who lost their child. Find a counselor or a trusted friend who can listen to your grief. This gives you an opportunity to process with someone who isn't closest to the one who has passed.

As we focus on self-care, we are able to process, not just the grief of loss, but also the magnification of other issues that come with loss. We are able to step back and see the big picture.

This perspective allows us to walk differently. We can give grace to others, grace to the family, grace to ourselves as we see shifts in personality and different responses to situations that previously may have had a different response.

Give yourself grace as you begin to understand and build your new *normal*. We don't have to engage in things that we once thought important, but now seem petty. We can truly see and enjoy life, because we have known death.

As you walk your grief journey, understand that you are changing. Death is going to magnify some aspects about who you are in a way that were previously hidden, but it will also open your eyes to the beauty of life.

Self-Care

Reflections	Questions
	What are some of the things that have been magnified in your life as a result your grandchild's death? *(Think about the positive things you saw magnified as well.)*
	What are some of the roles from the past that you feel like have returned? Are these roles positive or negative?
	In what ways do you need to self-care? Are there boundaries that you need to put in place to allow for you to be healthy?

SELF-CARE

Questions

With whom do you process your grief? Is this person a safe/healthy person? *(If you are processing this with your son/daughter who is the parent that lost the child, STOP. That is not healthy for either of you.)*

To whom do you need to offer grace? What is one way you can do that this next week?

In what areas of your life do you need to give yourself more grace?

How has your perspective on life changed since your grandchild's death? What is one thing you can do to capitalize on that perspective or shift from seeing the negative to seeing the positive?

Reflections

_____

_____

_____

_____

_____

_____

_____

_____

_____

_____

_____

_____

_____

_____

_____

_____

_____

_____

_____

_____

_____

TELLING YOUR STORY

TELLING YOUR STORY

Story Notes

——————————————————
——————————————————
——————————————————
——————————————————
——————————————————
——————————————————
——————————————————
——————————————————
——————————————————
——————————————————
——————————————————
——————————————————
——————————————————
——————————————————
——————————————————
——————————————————
——————————————————
——————————————————
——————————————————
——————————————————
——————————————————
——————————————————

Telling Your Story

Always be prepared to give the reason for the Hope you have.

I Peter 3:15

Telling your story of loss can be difficult and painful. Oftentimes, people find themselves trying to avoid sharing their story of loss because they are afraid if they do, then they are accepting their new reality. Many people feel shame and guilt surrounding their grandchild's death (and sometimes minimize their grief in comparison to that of their son or daughter); they can't bring themselves to share. Still others find it too painful, or they are afraid of the emotions they will feel and express as they share their story.

All these feelings are valid. Maybe you identify with more than one of these feelings. That's okay. We believe that sharing the story of your grandchild's death is an important step on your grief journey, but it is also something that should be treasured. We want to help you write your story.

We also want you to know that we understand the difficulty of this task, but remember that when you share your story in the group, you are sharing it with others who understand what you are feeling.

TELLING YOUR STORY

Pre-Writing

Here are some questions that we believe will help you write your story. Instead of readings this week, we want you to take time to write your story.

Oftentimes, some parts of our loss are hazy, or if we haven't told the story before, we share out of sequence, and then feel the need to go back and add in details. These questions will help you avoid feeling like you are all over the place when you write your story.

Don't leave this story writing till the last minute. We encourage you to begin early in the week to allow yourself the time you need to process through the story. Even if you have shared your story before, writing it down and working through the pre-writing questions will be very different than merely telling your story.

Pre-Writing:

- What is the last favorite memory you have of or with your grandchild?

- What sounds, smells, or sights do you clearly remember from the day of he or she passed? (Or of the day the accident resulting in terminal injury, or diagnosis of illness, etc.)

- What emotions took place inside of you (before and after the loss) that day?

Story Notes

_____

_____

_____

_____

_____

_____

_____

_____

_____

_____

_____

_____

_____

_____

_____

_____

_____

_____

TELLING YOUR STORY

Story Notes

_____
_____
_____
_____
_____
_____
_____
_____
_____
_____
_____
_____
_____
_____
_____
_____
_____
_____
_____
_____
_____

PreWriting

- Who are the key people you remember being present or a part of your loss that day?

- What are the key moments of the day(s) of your loss that you never want to forget?

- What is the sequence of how things happened?

- What lies has the enemy tried to get you to believe, regarding your loss that bring about fear, guilt, or shame? (Take time to prayerfully ask God this question.)

- What truth does God want you to know as you spend time writing your story? (Take time to prayerfully ask Him this question.)

Writing Your Story:

The preparation questions are meant to help you gather your thoughts together before you begin writing your story.

As you write your story, there are three main parts that you want to split it into. You do not need to include all the details in every part, but include enough to help the story flow and provide the necessary information for others to follow along.

(The side notes are for you to jot down notes about your story to help you write/type it out later.)

TELLING YOUR STORY

Writing Your Story

Before the loss:

- Include some biographical details for context (other grandchildren, did you live close, how often did you interact with your grandchild, etc.)

- Share what led up to the loss (ex. if your grandchild died from a terminal illness include when illness was discovered, his/her fight with illness, etc.)

- Be sure not to include too many details that would cause you to lose your listener's/reader's attention

The loss/death:

- *Share as much about the loss as you feel comfortable with. It doesn't need to be long, but if the death is a quick five to six word sentence, your listener/reader will be confused*

After loss:

- Share emotions/feelings you felt afterwards

- You can include some of the funeral, or memorial service preparations if you would like, but don't feel like you need to focus on that

- In what ways did you help the parents (your son/daughter and daughter-in-law/son-in-law)?

Story Notes

_____
_____
_____
_____
_____
_____
_____
_____
_____
_____
_____
_____
_____
_____
_____
_____
_____
_____
_____
_____
_____
_____

TELLING YOUR STORY

Story Notes

_____
_____
_____
_____
_____
_____
_____
_____
_____
_____
_____
_____
_____
_____
_____
_____
_____
_____
_____
_____

Writing Your Story

- Did you delay grieving the loss of your grandchild? (If so, how long and why did you feel you had to delay?)
- What was your support like? What was the most helpful support?
- Share where you are now and a little about where you would like to go

Again, we know how difficult this task can be. Our goal is to help you share your story in such a way that you have confidence to do so. Take your time with this and process through your emotions and feelings.

Write your Story:

Now, using your pre-writing questions and your story notes, take the time to write your story. Take as much time as you need to do this. If this is the first time you are telling your loss story, give yourself grace.

You may want to type it or write on a separate piece of paper.

If you are going through this workbook as part of a group, we'll be sharing these stories the next time we get together.

If you are doing this study on your own, find someone who you can trust to share your story with. Sharing your story may seem scary or hard, but sharing your story is an important part of your healing.

TELLING YOUR STORY

Use the Space Below to Outline Your Story if Needed

Story Notes

_____

_____

_____

_____

_____

_____

_____

_____

_____

_____

_____

_____

_____

_____

_____

_____

_____

_____

_____

_____

_____

CONFIDENCE

STORY
Debbie's Story

Our first-born daughter, Katy was born after six years of infertility. She has always been such a joy to my husband and me. She loves children, and we knew she would have many of her own one day. She prayed every Sunday at church that the Lord would send her siblings, and her prayers were answered with a brother and sister after twelve more years of infertility.

She married a wonderful Christian young man named Dennis, that my pastor husband led to Christ on one of his nights on outreach. Five years later she gave birth to our first grandson, Jonah. A couple of years later, came Peyton our first granddaughter.

As the Lord blessed, we received a second granddaughter, Kylie Noel. She was born shortly after Christmas. But this little girl was a magical little soul. She was tiny and looked just like her daddy. I was able to be the first one to hold her after the parents, in a quiet empty hallway. Her eyes locked in on mine and there was a special love and ache I felt in my heart so deep it took my breath away. I did not understand it all then, but I would one day.

Dennis and Katy lived a mile and a half from us, so it was fun to be able to see Kylie and her siblings as often as I wished. She even attended one of our women's retreats that I led, and she was comfortable in each ladies' arms that held her. Most mentioned how her constant gaze in their eyes was so unusual and captivating.

My husband and I were on our way home late one evening on Saturday, May 3rd, 2014, from a visit in the country with my parents. We got home and began to unpack and rest for the worship service the next day. My phone began to ring, and I saw it was my son-in-law calling. I picked it up, greeting him with a happy hello. The only words he was physically able to respond with were, *"Mom, Kylie is gone. She has died."* We would later learn that she had died of Sudden Infant Death Syndrome (SIDS). I could barely breathe to even respond. I just told him we would be right over.

I turned to my husband and began to cry as I told him the news. We both jumped into the truck and began the drive to their home. I screamed out my words uncontrollably, *"Robert, I will not be able to handle this."* I just could not believe that our 4-month-old beautiful, healthy little Kylie Noel was gone. No more chances that maybe she would be revived. It was over.

I kept telling him, *"I can't do this."* What will I say to my own child who has just lost her little baby girl? Or the firefighter Daddy who had performed CPR on his own child? My husband, in the middle of his own shock and grief, looked at me and said, *"Debbie, we either believe the Gospel is real or we don't. This is where God promises He will walk with us. He will be our strong tower. His Spirit will help us to do what we must do. And He will help our kids to do the same. We either believe it or not. We preach and teach that over and over to those around us. This is where the rubber meets the road. And I choose to believe and let Him do His work in our hearts and theirs."* Robert then prayed with me, and we pulled up in front of their house, where police cars, an ambulance, and fire trucks were gathered.

STORY

And as promised, we stepped onto their driveway full of God's truth. His Spirit moved through us and around us that night, and the days that followed. It was like a protective bubble. I even watched my heartbroken husband preach his own little grand-baby's funeral. And then saw several people make decisions to follow the same Jesus that we had known and trusted.

When we showed up, God was already there, filling us and our children with the energy for the next step. It was not easy. Sometimes the grief was excruciating, and I prayed often that they would not be wounded beyond any help. But each time we reached up, He was reaching down with comfort and healing.

And our hope to this day is: each day is one day closer to us holding her once again.

Blessed is a man who remains steadfast under trial, for when
he has stood the test he will receive the crown of life, which
God has promised to those who love Him.

-James 1:12 (ESV)

STORY

Reflections

Questions

How does Debbie's story relate to your story? How is it different?

What is something encouraging that you see in Debbie's story? How can you use that to help you move forward on your grief journey?

SELF-CARE

Scripture

10 Finally, be strong in the Lord and in the strength of his might. **11** Put on the whole armor of God, that you may be able to stand against the schemes of the devil. **12** For we do not wrestle against flesh and blood, but against the rulers, against the authorities, against the cosmic powers over this present darkness, against the spiritual forces of evil in the heavenly places. **13** Therefore take up the whole armor of God, that you may be able to withstand in the evil day, and having done all, to stand firm. **14** Stand therefore, having fastened on the belt of truth, and having put on the breastplate of righteousness, **15** and, as shoes for your feet, having put on the readiness given by the gospel of peace. **16** In all circumstances take up the shield of faith, with which you can extinguish all the flaming darts of the evil one; **17** and take the helmet of salvation, and the sword of the Spirit, which is the word of God, **18** praying at all times in the Spirit, with all prayer and supplication.

Ephesians 6:10-18a (ESV)

Reflections

_____

_____

_____

_____

_____

_____

_____

_____

_____

_____

_____

_____

_____

_____

_____

_____

_____

_____

Soul-Care

Reflections

_____

_____

_____

_____

_____

_____

_____

_____

_____

_____

_____

_____

_____

_____

_____

_____

_____

_____

_____

_____

Devotional Thought

Have you ever tried running in sand? It's not easy. It takes more effort to run in sand than it does to run on grass or concrete.

Think about times when you were younger and you were walking in sand, maybe it was at a playground, the beach, or maybe where you live is very sandy. As you step, your foot displaces sand, requiring extra effort to walk because you stepping on firm ground.

The Ephesians passage talks about putting on the armor of God. In this passage, the word *stand* is used several times. This means that the idea of standing is an important one to the thoughts in these verses.

In order to for us to stand well, we need to stand on truth. We talked about truth bringing us freedom in the previous chapter; it's also something that can give us firm ground to stand on.

Truth becomes a ground that we can, not only stand on, but we can also build our lives on it. Truth is something that we can come back to over and over again when we are struggling with doubt.

We can be confident when we know that the ground we stand on is true. Confidence helps us stand; truth is what we stand upon, and we can do so victoriously.

SOUL-CARE

Devotional Thought

It might seem strange to us that we can think about standing in confidence in the aftermath of the death of our grandchild, but we can. The truth is that, while we miss him/her, we know the truth that God is with us in the midst of that pain.

He will guide us on our grief journey, if we let Him. He may feel distant, or we may be upset with Him for allowing this tragedy to come into our lives, but He is always there for us. We just have to choose to look to Him.

For those who have spent time in the church, this passage of scripture is familiar. The armor of God is often used as a passage that helps teach us how to walk out our faith in God. It's a great tool.

As you think about this passage, remember that the reason we have the armor of God is to stand against the evil one, Satan. He is our true enemy in all of this. He is the one who brought death into the world. He is also the one who does not want us to stand in truth.

The good news is...you don't have to listen to him. You can stand firm against him in confidence. That confidence is found in God, in a personal relationship with Jesus. He is the one that can help you stand victoriously against the enemy.

Reflections

_____
_____
_____
_____
_____
_____
_____
_____
_____
_____
_____
_____
_____
_____
_____
_____
_____
_____

SOUL-CARE

Reflections

Questions

What is a truth that you have stood on in the midst of your grandchild's death? How has that helped you stand firm? If you are not sure you have one, ask God to show you a truth that you can stand on. How might that truth make a difference in your life as you move forward on your grief journey?

Have there been times during your grief journey that have felt like you are walking in sand or possibly standing in quick sand? How have you felt during those times? What has helped you get out of that? (If you feel like you're still in one of those times, what is a truth that you know that can help you stand firm?)

How have you been confident in moving forward on your grief journey? Is there something that you have held onto that has been of comfort? If not, what do you think it might take for you to confidently move forward on your grief journey?

SELF-CARE

Wind and Trees
Jeff Rollins

Between 1987 and 1991, Biosphere 2 was constructed. It was to be a scientific experiment that would research the viability of colonizing outer space through self-contained biospheres. It was made up of seven biome areas that were isolated from the outside world, a rainforest, ocean, mangrove wetlands, savannah grassland, a fog dessert, and two anthropogenic biomes for the scientists. While there have been no new space colonies as a result of Biosphere 2, which was one of the goals of the experiment, there were interesting scientific discoveries that were made while the experiments were being conducted.

Being a self-contained biome, Biosphere 2 afforded scientists the opportunity to study plant growth without the various factors that those plants might face in the wild. As I was doing research on trees and their root systems for our Hope Family Retreats, I came across some interesting information regarding trees in the rainforest biome.

The first interesting fact was that trees would grow more quickly in Biosphere 2 than their counterparts in the wild. In other words, the growth rate of trees was accelerated because of the self-contained environment they were growing in. The trees didn't have to deal with the changes in rainfall, climate extremes, etc. They were afforded the best growing environment with no adversity.

Secondly, I discovered that, despite the increased rate of growth, trees never reached full maturity. Scientists discovered that when the trees reached a certain height or weight, they would collapse and die. It was later found that this was caused by a lack of wind in the biosphere.

Inadvertently, scientists discovered that wind plays a crucial role in the growth and maturing of trees. While the growing conditions for the trees was optimal in the self-contained biome, the conditions needed for maturing were not. The absence of wind prevented trees from being able to mature into their full potential. The inability to fully mature was due to the trees being unable to develop reaction wood or stress wood.

Simply put, when wind blows in the wild it causes the trees to bend and sway. This bending causes the trees to produce stress wood (via changes on the cellular level), which is stronger than the regular wood on a tree. The absence of the wind does not allow for the development of stress wood, which makes the tree weaker.

Immediately, I saw a parallel to our lives. While all of us would like to live in a self- contained bubble that prevents us from having stress, suffering, or pain, that is not what is best for us. We grow and mature because we face and overcome conflicts, problems, and stress.

The absence of struggles in life is not something that helps, but rather hinders our maturity. We may feel comfortable in the absence of struggle, but that absence doesn't allow us to produce our own

SELF-CARE

stress wood that allows us to become stronger and mature.

For many, the days after their grandchild's death are uncertain. Most cannot think about the next day, much less, the next month or year. It isn't because they are trying to avoid them, but instead, many of the surviving loved ones have a deep longing to be reunited with the one who has passed. This doesn't mean that a person is suicidal, but rather that their grief is expressing itself in that deep desire to see their loved one again. This is a normal feeling after the loss of a loved one, and in many ways can be a healthy expression of grief. *(A continued dwelling on that desire to die and be reunited with a loved one isn't healthy.)*

Moving forward through the pain and grief of loss can cause someone to grow stronger. Much like the wind that produces the stress wood in trees, the tragedy of death can strengthen a person. However, it does come at a great cost. Moving forward requires walking into your pain; it doesn't mean forgetting about and not dealing with the feelings of loss.

Walking through the pain of loss allows us to grow stronger. Whether you realize it or not, you are stronger than you were before the death of your grandchild. You may not like that or it may not feel good, but you are still here, you are still going, and you are working through this book. You are stronger!

Because we have faced death and are still standing, we have shown the ability to face the winds of life and stand strong. We know we will not topple over because we have already stood strong. We are rooted in truth and faith.

Perhaps you have heard people share with others that, *"God will not give you more than you can handle."* While that is a well-intentioned statement, it's simply not true. The death of a grandchild is more than anyone can handle!

God allows us to experience more than we think we can handle because it causes us to go to Him for our strength. When we walk through more than we can handle, He strengthens us. He allows more than we can handle because when we walk through the tough times with Him, we can look back and see how He has strengthened us.

God is the one that can help us develop the *stress wood* in our lives that will help us move forward on our grief journey. He is the one that can hold us up in the face of life's wind, because, as our losses clearly remind us, we don't live in a bubble.

Self-Care

Questions	Reflections

Questions

What are some things that have helped you develop "stress wood" in your life? *(Don't think of just your grandchild loss, there could be other circumstances as well.)*

How do you look to God for strength in the middle of your circumstances? What has/hasn't worked for you in the past? What do you want to continue/change moving forward?

When you think of God giving you more than you can handle in order to cause you to trust in Him, how does that make you feel? Do you feel like you can trust God to help you through? Why/Why not?

Reflections

LOVE

STORY
JERRY'S STORY

Our first grandchild, John McDowell Allen IV (LJ), was born on October 9th, at 26 weeks. He came fourteen weeks prior to his expected due date. At birth, he weighed a mere 31 ounces, and was immediately moved into a neonatal intensive care unit (NICU). Each day brought an additional glimmer of hope that LJ would survive, even though his prognosis was guarded, at best.

As an indicator of his mini-stature, my favorite picture of him shows his parents' wedding rings used as bracelets on his tiny wrist. He spent virtually his entirely too short life in a NICU incubator, being removed only on his 17th day of life to let his parents hold him as he breathed his final breath in their arms.

I cannot imagine the anguish his parents felt as they drove home from the NICU after handing LJ back to the NICU nurses that horrible morning. They called me from the car at about 6:30 am letting me know the terrible news. It was my responsibility to tell my wife; how could I deliver such devastation? Mustering my utmost sympathy, I held her as she poured out her grieving tears.

As *the man of the family*, it was my role to be the strong shoulder on which to lean and cry, one which I was more than willing to accept and carry out. The big question, though, was how to do that through and despite of my own grief. At age 54, I was relatively well educated, experienced in business and life in general, but had no idea how to deliver whatever my family might need in this situation.

While I was starting to process my feelings about my own loss, I found it hard to fathom the loss my daughter and son-in-law would be experiencing. This was their first child; after so much anticipation about starting their family, what might they be feeling about this loss? What could I possibly say or do to help alleviate their despair? Knowing my own love for our two daughters and that I would do anything in my power to protect and care for them, how do I support and counsel them through the times ahead?

Supporting my wife was another role for which I was somewhat unprepared. I knew she was experiencing the grief of losing her first grandchild as well as the loss our daughter was feeling; being sensitive to her needs was critical. The incidence of divorce runs high in families who lose a child*; I was determined not to let that happen in our family. How to do that was an entirely unknown quantity.

While this wound was still fresh, I decided it would be best for me to try to suppress my own feelings of loss in order to be more supportive of and helpful to my daughter and wife. Fortunately, listening just happens to be one of my better skills; it certainly was critical in this situation. In most cases, it was better to simply support, listen and hold – words of advice would be of little value at this time, even if I would have had the right thing to say. There would be nothing I could say that would *"make it better"*; the best answer was simply to *"be there"*.

---

*While this is a common thought, and sometimes shared along with statistics, there have been no studies that have shown this to be the case. See ***https://www.compassionatefriends.org/to-the-newly-bereaved/***

STORY

One of the things that hit me hardest was the *"double"* grief I felt – my own loss about LJ, but, more importantly, the loss my daughter was feeling and how do I support and counsel her. While LJ was only with us for seventeen days, I had more than twenty-four years of life with her. Seeing her anguish over this tragedy wrenched at my heart as only a parent can understand. Again, a shoulder on which to cry, hugs and an open ear seemed to be the best I could offer – and, in the long run, turned out to be the best solution.

We got through the toughest times early on, even though today (twelve years after LJ's death) we all still have a tough time in October. It is something that I don't want to forget – how could you try to erase the memory of your grandson from your experiences. I still visit his gravesite by myself from time to time to sit quietly with him, cry, ask for his oversight to help me be the spouse, father and grandfather that I should be, and let him know I will be with him soon enough to play all the games that I play now with his siblings and cousins.

Long story short, no human can know how to "fix" losses like this. Simply being there and offering open arms and a shoulder on which to cry may be the best we can offer those in the throes of this kind of loss and suffering. We will never know what that might mean to somebody else; just be ready to be there.

PS – now for *"the end of the story"*. While losing LJ was and is excruciatingly sad, this is a tragedy-to-triumph story. During LJ's hospital stay, in order to keep the large circle of friends (over 300 people daily) updated, our daughter and her husband started a blog which eventually reached over 1500 people on five continents. Via a friend-of-a-friend, a young lady (who had been adopted herself and was now pregnant) was put in touch with our daughter to discuss adopting her soon-to-be newborn. Long story short, all agreed to this adoption, and infant Grace Caroline joined our family two days after LJ's original due date. Nothing can *"replace"* LJ; we continue to mourn his passing, but are eternally grateful for Grace's arrival. God does work in mysterious ways – we just need to have faith in Him that He knows what is best for us.

SOUL-CARE

Reflections

Questions

How does Jerry's story relate to your story? How is it different?

What is something encouraging that you see in Jerry's story? How can you use that to help you move forward on your grief journey?

STORY

Scripture

Reflections

The following is a paraphrase of Psalm 139. Before you read it, pray and ask God to speak it over you as you read. They are his words for you. Take time to let the words soak in.

1 My child, I know everything there is to know about you.

2 I perceive every movement of your heart and soul,
   and I understand your every
      thought before it even enters
      your mind.

3-4 I am so intimately aware of you, my child.
   I read your heart like an open book
   and I know all the words you're about to speak
   before you start a sentence!
I know every step you will take before your journey even begins.

5 I've gone into your future to prepare the way,
   and in kindness I follow behind you
   to spare you harm from your past.
   With my hand of love upon your life,
   I impart a blessing to you.

6 I know that this is just too wonderful, deep, and incomprehensible!
   My understanding of you brings you wonder and strength.

SOUL-CARE

Reflections	Scripture

Scripture

7 Where could you go from my Spirit?
   Where could you run and hide from
      my face?

8 If you go up to heaven, I'm there!
   If you go down to the realm of the
      dead, I'm there too!

9 If you fly with wings into the shining
      dawn, I'm there!

   If you fly into the radiant sunset, I'm
      there waiting!

10 Wherever you go, my hand will guide
      you;
   my strength will empower you.

11 It's impossible to disappear from me
      or to ask the darkness to hide you,
   for my presence is everywhere,
   bringing light into your night.

12 There is no such thing as darkness
      with me.
   The night, to me, is as bright as
      day;
   there's no difference between the
      two.

13 I formed your innermost being,
      shaping your delicate inside and
      your intricate outside,
   and wove them all together in your
      mother's womb.

Soul-Care

| Scripture | *Reflections* |

Scripture

14   I have made you so mysteriously
        complex, my child, I know your
        gratitude.
     You know that all I do is
        marvelously breathtaking.

15   I even formed every bone in your
        body
     when I created you in the secret
        place,
     carefully, skillfully shaping you
        from nothing to something.

16   I saw who I created you to be before
        you became you!
     Before you'd ever seen the light
        of day, the number of days I
        planned for you were already
        recorded in my book.

17-18 Every single moment I am thinking
        about you!
     Consider how precious and
        wonderful it is
     that I cherish you constantly in my
        every thought!
     My child, my desires toward you
        are more than the grains of sand
        on every shore!
     When you awake each morning, I
        am still with you.

                         Psalm 139:1-18

          (Paraphrased from TPT by Jeff Rollins)

Reflections

SOUL-CARE

Reflections

_____

_____

_____

_____

_____

_____

_____

_____

_____

_____

_____

_____

_____

_____

_____

_____

_____

_____

_____

_____

Questions

Take some time and let the paraphrase of Psalm 139 soak in. If you have to, reread it asking God to 'speak it' over you. What do you feel when you read it?

What is the most encouraging part the Psalm for you? Why?

What is the most difficult part of the Psalm for you to believe? Why?

SELF-CARE

How Grief Changes Over Time
Jeff Rollins

Think about the moment you learned that your grandchild had passed away. Or perhaps the more difficult day is when he or she received a diagnosis of a terminal illness, or the accident that would eventually take your grandchild's life. Maybe it was when your son or daughter told you that you were going to have a grandson or granddaughter (perhaps the first), only to find out later that the mom had miscarried or your grandchild was stillborn.

Whatever way you look at it, there is a moment in time when the reality of death hit you hard. Perhaps you felt like you had the wind knocked out of you by a cruel punch in your gut, or maybe you felt like you wanted to go to sleep and never wake up. For some, the feeling is as though there's an incredibly heavy weight on their shoulders that doesn't seem like it will ever be lifted.

That's what many people feel like when their loved one dies. It's what your grandchild's parents felt knowing that their child was no longer here. In that, so many are left with the weight of a heavy question: *Will I always feel this way?*

As a grandparent walking through the loss of a grandchild, you might have asked that question or perhaps are still asking that question. It's a normal question to ask, and it is also a good question to ask. However, immediately after the loss, there is no way that you can truly know the answer to that question.

The answer, however, is that you don't always have to feel the way you felt right after your loss.

Grief will never go away; that's the bad news. The good news is the way we carry our grief can change over time. As we walk our grief journey and take those difficult steps forward, we will begin to heal. Healing doesn't mean that we forget our pain, but rather that we are able to think of the death of our grandchild without heaviness of grief. We are able to remember good times we had before the loss. We are able to laugh. We are able to do the things that at the beginning seemed hard or unimaginable. We begin to get stronger, but the grief we feel over the loss will never completely go away.

In a way, that grief is a reminder of the love that we have for him or her. Jamie Anderson, the author of *Doctor Who*, said it this way: *"Grief, I've learned, is really just love. It's all the love you want to give, but cannot. All that unspent love gathers up in the corners of your eyes, the lump in your throat, and in that hollow part of your chest. Grief is just love with no place to go."*

And while it is true that grief doesn't ever go away; it does change. The question then becomes, how does grief change?

Many people believe that over time, grief fades and becomes smaller and smaller. The idea behind that is that as you continue to live, your grief will lessen. It's the false idea that time heals

SELF-CARE

all wounds.

Time doesn't heal all wounds, nor does our grief get smaller with time. In an article on the blog page, *What's Your Grief,* the author references Dr. Lois Tonkin with the idea that we grow around our grief, rather than our grief becoming smaller.

Simply put, our grief doesn't get smaller or lessen as time passes, but rather our lives grow and our experiences expand. This causes the grief we experience to become proportionally less of our lives with time.

The illustration of the ball with the jars, which the article borrows from another website, shows a

People tend to believe that grief shrinks over time

What really happens is that we grow around our grief

good example of the false view of grief lessening with time, and the more accurate view of how we grow around our grief.

As we move forward on our grief journey, we experience more of life and that grows around our

SELF-CARE

grief, rather than our grief shrinking.

Another way to understand how grief changes is similar to how our perception of time changes for us as we get older. When we are five years old, one year is the equivalent to twenty percent (20%) of the life we have lived, and one month is the equivalent of one about 1/60 of our lives. When we are ten years old, one year is the equivalent of ten percent (10%) of our lives, and one month is the equivalent of 1/120 of our lives. When we turn forty, one year becomes two and half percent (2.5%) of our lives, and one month is 1/480 of our lives. As we continue to live, the percent one year is in our life continues to lessen.

The amount of time that makes up one year and one month never changes, it is always 365 days (366 in a leap year), 52 weeks, or twelve months, but the amount of times we experience months and years increases, which makes each of those units of time a smaller portion of our lives. Time doesn't change, but as we move forward, with time, our perception of time changes.

That is, in essence, what happens with grief as we walk our journey. As we continue to move forward, we begin to establish a new normal. Our life experiences extend beyond the grief that covered our entire life experience at the time of our grandchild's death. We meet new people, make new friends, establish new routines, etc.

The key is to move forward. Grief will never change if we attempt to hold on to the way life was prior to our loss. The reality is, there will be friendships that will fade away as we walk our grief journey. There will be places we routinely visited that we will no longer frequent. There will be traditions that we no longer hold or participate in. There is nothing wrong with that change. Grief is a change. It changes nearly everything and it affects all of our life moving forward. Similarly, there will be new friendships, places, routines, traditions, etc.

However, if we try to make things go back to the way they were, we keep our jars from getting bigger. In other words, we keep from growing around our grief. When this happens, we do not open ourselves to new experiences, we do not open ourselves to new relationships, we do not open ourselves up to new places or routines, etc. In essence we turn our backs on the world outside of us, and focus on our grief believing that the ball will get smaller or go away. Trying to return the jar back to the way it was before loss will keep our grief from changing, and we will get stuck in our grief.

I am not saying that you have to make drastic changes to your life after the loss of a grandchild. Rather, I am saying that it's important to be open possible changes, positive and negative.

As you grow, you begin to figure out what your new normal will be and you continue to move forward. As you move forward, your grief will change, and you will change. As that happens, the way you carry your grief changes, but it doesn't go away. Instead, you grow around your grief into a stronger and more capable person.

SELF-CARE

Reflections

Questions

What are some of the new experiences you have had since your loss? How are you growing in those changes?

How does the idea of your grief never going away make you feel? How can that idea help you grow?

SELF-CARE

Questions

How did the explanation of how grief changes over time help you understand your grief?

What things do you see that are causing or could cause you to get stuck on your grief journey? How can you change/avoid them?

Reflections

_____

_____

_____

_____

_____

_____

_____

_____

_____

_____

_____

_____

_____

_____

_____

_____

_____

_____

_____

_____

_____

_____

_____

PURPOSE

STORY
Julie's Story

The Lord has blessed us eight times with precious grandchildren. Each unique and a special gift that I am thankful for in so many ways. They call me Granna! No matter where I am or how I feel, hearing that name lights up my world. Devastatingly, I have not been able to hear our third grandchild Samuel call me Granna yet. He went to be with the Lord shortly after his birth. So, for now, I have to wait to hear that sweet sound from him.

Losing Samuel caused an indescribable pain, heart break and sorrow. Our son and daughter-in-law, Edwin and Jessica, received Samuel's prognosis at 20 weeks. I prayed, pleaded, felt helpless, distraught, shed countless tears.

All the emotions and grief of losing a grandchild, compounded as you watch your own child and his wife go through the unimaginable pain caused by the loss of a child, this was a grief that was more immense than I had ever experienced in my life. I remember being so numb with grief all I could repeat in my prayers was Thank You Lord, not knowing what or how to pray, I just had to trust. Of course, I would never choose the outcome, but I know God can be trusted. His ways are higher than my own. (Isaish 55:8-9) Still that did not mean I understood it and that didn't mean the pain stopped.

I realize now, looking back, the prayers of Thank you Lord had purpose. I was thankful for God's presence in my life. Thankful for His presence in Edwin and Jessica's life. Grateful for the strength that the Lord gave them.

They were and are such a wonderful example of faith and strength. I am amazed at how they, as Samuel's parents, have honored Samuel then and now. I am thankful for the knowledge and hope we have in Christ that no matter how short our time with Samuel here was, we will be with him in our eternal home in Heaven.

Missing Samuel is always something that will be with us but we move forward keeping in mind we will be with Samuel in Heaven. For now we do our best here and find ways to honor his memory. For me personally that involved a silly little orange plastic bracelet I slipped on my wrist that George and Olivia (his older siblings) won at a visit to Chuck E Cheese while Jessica was in the hospital after Samuel's birth. It somehow helped. Each time I would look at it I felt a peace, a calm, a connection to Samuel....a reminder of him and the Hope we have for a time to come when we will meet again. So, I turned that silly bracelet into a more permanent bracelet, I add a bead to it each year on Samuel's birthday (in his colors – orange and blue) You won't ever see me without that bracelet.

I've done small acts of kindness quietly, thinking of him- just small things. As a family, we have established a tradition in Samuel's memory. Yearly we pack Operation Christmas child boxes. His great Aunt Ginger and her late husband Arnold have had a passion for OCC boxes for years.

Story

Shortly after Samuel went to heaven they asked if we would be OK with packing boxes in Samuel's memory. WHAT A GREAT IDEA! Edwin, and Jessica agreed and so did I, so the tradition began. This year alone we all got together and packed 55 boxes around the kitchen table. Wow, that means 55 children from all parts of the world, along with their families, will experience the Love of Jesus thru those boxes because of Samuel. That just proves there is NO footprint so small that it does not leave an imprint on this world!

Samuel has made a big imprint on our world and he continues to make an imprint on the world as we honor his memory. We will carry on here until we meet in our eternal home in heaven. Where, when we meet there, I will no longer have to wait to hear that precious, third grandchild, Samuel call me Granna.

STORY

Reflections

Questions

How does Julie's story relate to your story? How is it different?

What is something encouraging that you see in Julie's story? How can you use that to help you move forward on your grief journey?

SOUL-CARE

Scripture

15 When Joseph's brothers saw that their father was dead, they said, "It may be that Joseph will hate us and pay us back for all the evil that we did to him." **16** So they sent a message to Joseph, saying, "Your father gave this command before he died: **17** 'Say to Joseph, "Please forgive the transgression of your brothers and their sin, because they did evil to you."' And now, please forgive the transgression of the servants of the God of your father." Joseph wept when they spoke to him. **18** His brothers also came and fell down before him and said, "Behold, we are your servants." **19** But Joseph said to them, "Do not fear, for am I in the place of God? **20** As for you, you meant evil against me, but God meant it for good, to bring it about that many people should be kept alive, as they are today.

Genesis 50:15-20 (ESV)

Reflections

Soul-Care

Reflections	Devotional Thought

Reflections

_____
_____
_____
_____
_____
_____
_____
_____
_____
_____
_____
_____
_____
_____
_____
_____
_____
_____
_____
_____
_____
_____

Devotional Thought

There's a difference between hurting and harming. It may not seem like there is a difference, and in many cases, the feelings from being hurt or harmed are very similar, if not the same. There is, however, a distinct difference.

In the Genesis passage, we see that Joseph knows that his brothers intended to harm him. That is, they did something that inflicted pain in order to damage Joseph.

(Here is a brief summary if you are unfamiliar with the story. Joseph's brothers were jealous of him and sold him into slavery, after deciding against killing him. God then raises Joseph up as second in command over Egypt. That position allows him to save his family during a severe famine.)

The difference between hurt and harm lies in the intent. Think about different situations in which you have experienced some sort of pain. Some of those situations are caused by someone trying to intentionally hurt us or cause us damage, some are caused by someone unintentionally hurting us, and others are caused by someone intentionally hurting us in order to heal us. In each situation we feel pain.

An example of harm could be the actions of someone who intentionally starts a rumor to damage our reputation. It could be a former classmate, a friend (or former friend), a relative, or even a coworker. The reason behind why the rumor is started isn't important in determining the intent of being harmed. What is important is that the person is intentionally trying to inflict pain.

Soul-Care

Devotional Thought

If you have ever participated in competitive sports, you have most likely experienced someone unintentionally hurting you. I remember one time that my son was playing baseball. He had walked and was at first base. The catcher tried to throw him out at first after a pitch, but his throw was off target. My son dove back to the base, but because the throw was off target, the first baseman ended up stepping on him with his cleats while attempting to catch the throw. There was nothing intentional by the first baseman, but the cleat marks on my son's side were the evidence of getting hurt.

I (Jeff) was experiencing some extreme pain in one of my molars a while back. The pain would come and go in waves. I ended up having to get an emergency root canal done. The dentist intentionally inflicted hurt upon me (anesthesia shot, drilling out the nerve, etc.), however the goal was that the hurt would heal me. The pain that I had been experiencing prior to having the procedure done was so bad that I was glad to experience the pain of the root canal.

Sometimes God allows for us to walk through pain and hurt. It is part of living in a world where death and sin are present. That is what you are walking through on the grief journey you are on. That hurt is what nearly everyone who has lost a loved one has to deal with. It does not mean that God caused it, but He has allowed it.

Your grandchild's death is painful. It hurts. It doesn't mean that the intent is to harm you. God does, however, want to use it

Reflections

_____

_____

_____

_____

_____

_____

_____

_____

_____

_____

_____

_____

_____

_____

_____

_____

_____

_____

SOUL-CARE

Reflections

_____
_____
_____
_____
_____
_____
_____
_____
_____
_____
_____
_____
_____
_____
_____
_____
_____
_____
_____
_____
_____

Devotional Thought

for good, your good, for the good of others. He wants to take the hurt and bring healing in your life and in the lives of others.

I don't know what that *good* looks like in your life, but I know that God won't push you to it, He wants to partner with you to bring it about. It takes a shift in perspective.

Joseph's brothers intended to harm him by selling him into slavery. They didn't just want to hurt him, they wanted to inflict that damage upon him. They wanted to get rid of him.

It took between 13 - 20 years (depending on who you talk to) for Joseph to go from slave to second in command in Egypt. At some point he was able to shift his perspective from focusing on the harm that his brothers had caused him to seeing the good that God was doing through him.

I believe God wants to do the same for you. Maybe you are already there and can see what God is doing, or maybe you have no clue and feel like you are still drowning in your grief. Either way, God is with you and wants to bring about good. It's who He is.

SOUL-CARE

Questions	Reflections

Questions

What are some ways that you have seen the difference between harm and hurt in your life? What have you learned (or can learn) from those situations?

What are some things that you can see God doing on your grief journey that are bringing about good? (If it is still really early on, try and imagine some good that you want to see come out of your grief journey.)

What is your role in the things you listed above?

Reflections

_____

_____

_____

_____

_____

_____

_____

_____

_____

_____

_____

_____

_____

_____

_____

_____

_____

_____

SELF-CARE

Walk Through the Pain
Mackenzie Rollins

The days and months that follow the loss of a grandchild are filled with difficult moments. The decision has to be made, almost daily, to continue to move forward. A choice must be made to walk into the pain of those difficult moments, and in doing so, begin the process of grief and healing.

Typically, we try to avoid pain; it's natural. Perhaps that is why most people say that the first stage of grief is denial. We don't want to feel pain because it's unpleasant and miserable at times. You didn't want to feel the pain of losing a grandchild. No one does. It is a reality we don't want to accept.

However, we need to accept it. There comes a point when all of us have to accept this new reality; we will have to carry the pain of loss with us the rest of our lives. We can't avoid it, we have to walk forward into that pain.

It is difficult. It is painful, and some days it just seems down right impossible. However, we must remember that pain is an indicator. It communicates to us that something is wrong. This is true of both physical and emotional pain. It is a message that causes us to react.

When we touch a hot stove and feel the pain our first reaction is to jerk away. Emotional pain has the same effect on us; however, we must respond differently to this type of pain. We must keep our hand "on the burner" and allow ourselves to experience the emotional pain. In doing so, we begin to move forward and we become healthier. We begin to heal.

When we avoid the emotional pain of loss, in a way we are trying to hold onto what once was, specifically that our grandchild is still with us. While this is a natural feeling, it will cause us to get stuck. The unfortunate truth is that he/she is no longer with us and we need to move forward into a new normal with that reality. We cannot do that if we avoid that pain.

It's hard. No one wants to do it, but we are not alone.

When we walk into the pain, we are able to invite God into our pain. When we take the honest truth of what we are feeling and experiencing to Him, He enters into that truth and reality with us, but He doesn't just sit there; He walks with us through that pain, shouldering the burden of grief when we feel like it is too much to carry.

Rather than backing away from the emotional pain that we feel as a result of our grandchild's death, we need to process it and move forward with it as a new reality in our lives. We have to choose to walk into the pain, because in doing so we can walk through the pain and continue living.

It is God who can help us to accept this as our new reality. He is also the one who walks with us through the pain into a place of healing; He continues to do so each day.

SELF-CARE

God also wants us to walk with others into their pain and through their pain, to a place of healing on the other side. He can use loss in our lives as a way to allow us to walk with others through the pain of losing their grandchild. It is a journey that begins with death, but can bring hope and healing amidst the loss.

We need to tell ourselves: I will walk into the pain, and I will walk through the pain, because by doing so, I won't get stuck in the pain.

SELF-CARE

Reflections

_____
_____
_____
_____
_____
_____
_____
_____
_____
_____
_____
_____
_____
_____
_____
_____
_____
_____
_____
_____
_____
_____
_____

Questions

Do you find yourself trying to avoid emotional pain or trying to walk through it? Has this been helpful to you? Do you need to change the way you approach your emotional pain? If so, how?

Because pain is an indicator of something that needs to be addressed, what might your pain be telling you? How do you need to address those things?

SELF-CARE

Questions

In what ways have you moved forward through your pain? If you feel like you haven't, what are some ways that you can begin to move forward through it?

What do you use as motivation to move forward? If you don't feel like you have something, what might be a good motivator for you? How has that helped (or could help) you on your grief journey?

Reflections

_____

_____

_____

_____

_____

_____

_____

_____

_____

_____

_____

_____

_____

_____

_____

_____

_____

_____

_____

_____

_____

MOVING
FORWARD

STORY
EVELYN'S STORY

On May, 15, 2010, my daughter, Sherry, her husband Steven, and their two daughters, Emma (eight) and Eiley (two and a half) left Katy, TX, to drive to New Orleans, LA to attend the ordination ceremony for Steven's brother at New Orleans Baptist Theological Seminary. A few miles past Grosse Tete, LA, the vehicle Steven was driving hit a pocket of water on I-10 and hydroplaned across the I-10 median into oncoming traffic. Their vehicle was hit by an 18-wheeler in the front passenger side. As a result of the accident, my granddaughter, Emma was killed, my daughter, Sherry suffered a severe head injury, a broken left arm and a crushed right pelvis. Steven suffered broken ribs and Eiley, who was strapped in her car seat behind Steven, suffered minor injuries.

I received a call from Steven around 2 pm that Saturday afternoon, that they had been in an accident and that he, Sherry and Eiley were being transported to a hospital in Baton Rogue. He said that Emma was being taken to a different hospital in Baton Rogue. He said that Sherry was moaning as she was put into the ambulance and that Emma was not saying much.

I, along with my oldest daughter and my oldest grandson, left for Baton Rouge as soon as we could that afternoon. On the drive to Baton Rogue, we received the call that Emma had died and that Sherry was in the intensive care unit. It is because of God's mercy that anyone survived the accident.

The following Monday, the hospital discharged Steven and Eiley. Steven stayed at the hospital to be with Sherry, and we brought Eiley back home to Katy.

We had to plan a funeral. God miraculously provided the funds to buy a cemetery plot and pay for a graveside funeral that was planned for the Thursday after the accident. With the help of other family members and close friends of Steven and Sherry, we made all the arrangements.

Steven drove home from Baton Rouge with his parents the next Thursday to attend the funeral. Steven's brother stayed at the hospital in Baton Rouge as Sherry was having surgery on her arm and pelvis. Steven and his parents drove back to Baton Rouge the next day.

Sherry stayed in ICU in Baton Rogue for six weeks before being transferred to TIRR Memorial Hermann Rehab Hospital in the Houston Medical Center. Six weeks later she was discharged from TIRR. Before leaving, Steven told her about the accident and Emma. My other two daughters and I were in the room when Steven told Sherry. I had been grieving the death of my granddaughter, but when I heard the wails and saw the grief of my daughter and Steven, it was almost more than I could bear. Steven and Sherry's grief is described in Matthew 2:18, "*A voice is heard in Ramah, weeping and great mourning, Rachel weeping for her children, and refusing to be comforted, because they were no more.*"

Emma had accepted Jesus Christ as her Lord and Savior and was baptized in October, 2008, so we know we will be reunited with her. She wanted to be a missionary. We heard stories of how she witnessed to some of her classmates in the third grade.

STORY

Our family clung to Romans 8:28, *"And we know that for those who love God all things work together for good, for those who are called according to his purpose."* There are no adequate words to describe how the body of Christ at Kingsland Baptist Church ministered to my family during this time. They are still ministering to us.

At the time of the accident, I lived with Sherry and Steven. I had moved in with them after Eiley was born, and took care of Eiley. We would go and walk home with Emma after school each day. God had placed me in their home knowing I would be needed to continue to care for Eiley as Sherry healed.

I stuffed a lot of my grief because there was a lot of work to do and I also did not want to add to Sherry and Steven's grief by grieving in front of them. Five years later, after my mother died, I attended Grief Share for the first time. I knew I had grief on top of grief. I was asked to become a Grief Share Facilitator a year later and I am still in the program. It has helped me with my healing and moving forward with my life. The deep grief I felt as I watched and heard Sherry and Steven grieve is the worst thing I have ever experienced in my life. Psalm 6:6-7, *"I am worn out from sobbing. All night, I flood my bed with weeping, drenching it with my tears. My vision is blurred by grief."*

The first year or two after Emma died, I was very busy taking care of Eiley and Sherry still had memory issues. She did not remember simple things but was able to go back to work. Her focus was much better at work. I was focused on helping her with simple chores around the house and trying to help lift the load of daily responsibilities as she healed from physical injuries. And then there were days when her grief surfaced in anger, slammed doors, loud sobs. My heart still grieved deeply for her. I do not have the words to adequately describe my grief other than it was deep. Steven was the driver and his grief was compounded. All I could do was pray without ceasing and cry out for His Grace and Mercy. What I did witness was that their marriage became even stronger as they depended on each other and most of all on our Father. As a grandparent, you grieve the death of the child, but you grieve even more at your child's grief.

Since Sherry's healing from the injuries from the accident, she and Steven have ministered to several families who had a child die suddenly in an accident. As they ministered to those families, their healing continued and continues to this day. 2 Corinthians 1:4, *"He comforts us in all our affliction, so that we may be able to comfort those who are in any kind of affliction with the comfort we ourselves receive from God."*

STORY

Healing and moving forward, for this grandmother, happens each time I can comfort someone who is grieving. The grief is very deep and I never want any of it to be wasted. The Father has allowed me to minister through Grief Share these past five years. The personal healing for me is beyond describing. As I grieve with others, the Holy Spirit comforts me in ways that are beyond my words to describe. Do I still grieve Emma? Yes, but thinking about that beautiful, red-headed, blue-eyed little girl brings a smile to my spirit and knowing that she will never have to experience this kind of deep grief gives me a lot of comfort.

STORY

Questions

How does Evelyn's story relate to your story? How is it different?

What is something encouraging that you see in Evelyn's story? How can you use that to help you move forward on your grief journey?

Reflections

_____

_____

_____

_____

_____

_____

_____

_____

_____

_____

_____

_____

_____

_____

_____

_____

_____

_____

_____

_____

SOUL-CARE

Reflections

_____
_____
_____
_____
_____
_____
_____
_____
_____
_____
_____
_____
_____
_____
_____
_____
_____
_____

Scripture

18 Remember not the former things,
      nor consider the things of old.

19 Behold, I am doing a new thing;
      now it springs forth, do you not
      perceive it?
    I will make a way in the wilderness
      and rivers in the desert.

20 The wild beasts will honor me,
      the jackals and the ostriches, for
    I give water in the wilderness,
      rivers in the desert,
      to give drink to my chosen
      people,

21 the people whom I formed for
      myself that they might declare
      my praise.

Isaiah 43:18-21 (ESV)

Soul-Care

Devotional Thought

God makes things new. He does not see us in our pain and leave us there. He does not see our circumstances and leave us to fend for ourselves. He is actively involved in always renewing or redeeming the things around us. If we let Him.

These verses talk about how God is on the verge of, or starting, something new for his people, the Israelites. As He talks about the new thing that He is doing, He paints a picture of creating water in a dry land, taking something as harsh and desolate as a desert and making it into something refreshing.

Oftentimes, our grief of loss leaves us feeling like we are in a desolate wasteland. We look around at the circumstances and situations that we find ourselves in and we wonder if things will ever get better. It's hard to think of life getting better because we don't see a way out of the situation or we don't believe that any good can come of this.

But God.

God is making something new out of our situations. He is redeeming the loss that we experience. He has refreshing care for us in the midst of the wasteland of grandchild loss. He has not abandoned us. We may not feel it, but He is doing something new. He is the one doing it.

Reflections

_____

_____

_____

_____

_____

_____

_____

_____

_____

_____

_____

_____

_____

_____

_____

_____

_____

_____

SOUL-CARE

Reflections

Devotional Thought

Our role is to partner with Him in that new thing he is doing. We may not understand it, and rarely will we ever fully understand what God asks us to do before we do it. However, our job is to trust Him and obey Him. He will do the rest.

When we partner with God and walk into the new thing that He is doing, we will show others how to do the same. We will create a path forward from the wastelands to the rivers, from despair to hope.

We are able to do it, not because we are strong, but because we have chosen to partner with a strong God. A God who makes things new.

SOUL-CARE

Questions	Reflections

Questions

What is the new thing that God is doing in your life? If you can't see it, what would you want him to do?

What are some things that have caused you to feel like you are in a wasteland? How have you dealt with those things?

What do you sense God is asking you to do in order to partner with Him as He makes something new out of your circumstances? How might that help others later on?

Reflections

_____
_____
_____
_____
_____
_____
_____
_____
_____
_____
_____
_____
_____
_____
_____
_____
_____
_____

SELF-CARE

Secondary Losses
Jeff Rollins

Naturally, the focus of our time has been spent on the loss of our grandchild, perhaps this is our primary loss, or perhaps this study has highlighted your grief of another loss (child, spouse, or parent). However, our grief is not limited to merely loss in terms of death. There are other losses that are painful as well. These losses, known as secondary losses, are the ones that we will continue to feel until we reunite with our grandchild.

A secondary loss is the loss of an activity, event, routine, etc. that will no longer occur because of the death of our loved one. They can be dreams that we had with our grandchild, vacations we wanted to go on, not getting to tuck them in at night when they spend the night at your house, no more first day of school pictures, that empty chair at the table during family gatherings, the missing person in the family picture, or even as simple as a text message that will never be read. Most likely, in your group discussion times, you will have touched upon some of these secondary losses.

The difficulty with these losses is that they can impact us when we least expect them to. They become part of the triggers that cause us to feel the pain of grief.

Triggers typically come from the traumatic moments in loss, but are also found in our secondary losses. People who have not experienced the loss of a loved one might not understand these triggers. In fact, when we are triggered and we respond with grief, they may think we are not *ok* or that we are slipping into a depression. It's because they don't understand our grief, and perhaps they may not trust our grief.

The Lord trusts us in our grief because He knows He is right there with us to help us through. Others don't necessarily trust our grief because they don't know this type of grief themselves. They care about and love us deeply, but they don't want us *feeling sad*.

The grief can be heavy or light depending on the trigger, or even our state of mind when we are triggered. Typically they can cause us to have a bad day or week, especially early on in our grief. Unfortunately, many people often mistake our secondary loss grief or our triggers for us not continuing to move forward.

These are the times when we need extra grace for others. They simply don't understand. Others don't know why it's so hard to move forward or think we are stuck because they don't understand that life will be filled with secondary losses that we will continually encounter.

SELF-CARE

While we can't avoid triggers or secondary losses, we can prepare for them. Here are some tips to help you navigate these times:

- ***Allow yourself to feel the pain:*** don't try to avoid the pain that is associated with that trigger or secondary loss; acknowledge it. Cry if you need to.

- ***Give yourself grace:*** this is a normal part of the grieving process, one that can't be avoided.

- ***Pick a verse:*** find a verse to cling to in those moments you are triggered, memorize it, or write it on a card and have it ready to read.

- ***Take a moment:*** pause for a moment to catch your breath. Taking a moment can allow you to reset. Take the time you need to recover.

Remember, this is a life long journey you are on. Triggers and secondary losses will always come, but you don't have to fear them. You will be prepared.

SELF-CARE

Reflections

Questions

What are some of the secondary losses that you have already seen in your life? How have you dealt with them?

Of the helpful tips, which one do you think you need most or is most helpful for you?

MOVING FORWARD

Questions

Over the course of the last few months, you have had the opportunity to walk through your grief. You have read stories of other grandparents who are walking a similar grief journey to yours.

Our prayer is that, while the stories may be different, you would not feel like you are alone in feeling the weight and pain of the death of your precious grandchild.

Take some time and go back and reread your story from earlier in the workbook. As you read, take some time to reflect on the following questions:

What **HOPE** do you have now as you continue to walk forward on your grief journey?

How has your **FAITH** grown as you have worked through the book?

What **TRUTH** has God impressed as you have read and answered questions?

Reflections

_____

_____

_____

_____

_____

_____

_____

_____

_____

_____

_____

_____

_____

_____

_____

_____

_____

_____

_____

_____

_____

_____

MOVING FORWARD

Reflections

_____

_____

_____

_____

_____

_____

_____

_____

_____

_____

_____

_____

_____

_____

_____

_____

_____

_____

_____

_____

_____

Questions

Where is your **CONFIDENCE** as you move forward on your grief journey?

How do you see God's **LOVE** at work in your grief?

What **PURPOSE** do you have, or want to have, as you move forward?

TRUE HOPE

TRUE HOPE

God's Design:

God created the world with beauty and order, free from death, pain, and suffering. We see it in the beauty of a sunset, we hear it in the song of a bird singing in the morning, we feel it in the hug of a loved one. God put these into His design for the world.

He also created us for relationship, to be in relationship with family, our friends, different communities, but also with Him. God loves us and desires a relationship with us.

Unfortunately, something happened that took us out of that design. When Adam and Eve sinned, we stepped out of God's design and find ourselves in the brokenness of the world we currently live in.

That brokenness came into the world through sin, and with that sin came death. (Romans 5:12) We don't like to talk about sin or to look at sin as the reason for the brokenness in the world, but the truth is that the Bible tells us that sin entered the world and death entered through that sin.

Brokenness:

Sin, as one author states, is the attempt to meet a legitimate need in an illegitimate way. Sometimes can find ourselves in situations where we are attempting to that very thing. This is because we are living in brokenness, not God's design, so we try to meet needs in our own way.

We live in brokenness. It affects everything about our lives, our relationships, our thoughts, our actions, and even the actions of others towards us. The reason for this is because we're all sinners. (Romans 3:23)

The death of our loved one is a part of that brokenness. We can see the brokenness of the world in insensitive things people say to us, relationships that are strained, the inability to converse about differing ideas, unforgiveness, and so many other things.

Far too often, we try to escape the pain and brokenness by denial or numbing. We self medicate because we don't want to feel the way we do. However, it does not satisfy our need to escape the pain, and oftentimes leads us into more brokenness.

We try to overcome that pain by working hard, taking up a cause that we think will give our loss, or even ourselves, purpose. We may devote ourselves to raising awareness or money in favor of a cause, to support research to combat a specific disease, or issue. These are good things, but unfortunately they can become burdensome if the goal of doing them is to find purpose or escape the pain and brokenness of life. These worthy endeavors, while good and worthwhile, cannot take us out of the brokenness of this world or fill the emptiness we feel inside of us.

At other times we even turn to religion or doing good works to try to heal the pain and brokenness we feel in our lives. We attend church thinking that going there will help us escape. We volunteer and serve others with that same desire. However, while those things may help us feel better or possibly encourage us, we still find ourselves living in a broken world with pain and suffering; they not allow for us to escape.

Ultimately, our attempts to escape are our efforts to overcome sin. None of these attempts work. We find ourselves stuck in the brokenness of sin and in a world suffering under its consequences.

That sin ultimately separated us from God and took us out of God's design for the world. We have a deep, innate longing to return to that design, free from the brokenness of this world.

However, God knew all this would happen. Because of this, He made a way for us to return back to His design. He gave us a true hope.

True Hope:

God's design for true hope is found in His son Jesus. God is not a god who is foreign to grief and brokenness. He experienced it firsthand when He sent His son to earth.

Jesus came to earth and lived a life that was without sin. He didn't participate in the brokenness of this world by His own actions, but He experienced that brokenness at the hands of others; He was despised and rejected, He experienced death (His father, Joseph died before His ministry began), He was denied by His closest friends, and even falsely accused, beaten, and executed. He experienced all this willingly, for us.

He went through all that without sin. He died on the cross to pay for our sins. He took upon Himself the brokenness that we should rightfully pay for. However, he didn't stay dead.

Jesus rose from the dead and defeated the power of death. His death and resurrection is our true hope. The hope that we can return back to God's design for this world. The hope that we will one day be reunited with our loved ones who have passed, the hope that, while we live in this broken world, we don't have to live in that brokenness in our own lives.

In order to return back to God's design, we must *repent* and *believe*. We repent of our sins, asking Jesus to forgive us, and we confess Him as Lord of our lives, surrendering our own plan for our lives for His plan, and asking Him to give us the strength to live for Him.

Returning to God's design allows us to not just survive in this world, but to thrive and it can be done with a simple prayer. A prayer that is the beginning of living your life in God's design. The goal is not to change your eternal destiny (although that is a part of it), but rather to return back to God's design for your life now.

The Decision:

If you would like to return to God's design you can pray the prayer below. We encourage you to do it aloud.

Jesus, I need you.
Forgive me of my sins and save me.
Come into my life and guide me.
I confess you as the Lord of my life.

While there is nothing magical about those words, your heart is the key. This is the beginning of your new life in God's Design, living with Him.

Thriving:

In God's Design, despite living in a broken world, He created us to thrive!

He does not see our circumstances as what define us. To Him, we are not a person who has lost a child, a sibling, a spouse, a grandchild, or someone we love. While that may be part of our story, it does not define who we are in His eyes. He sees us as more than our circumstances, or our day to day struggles.

God looks at us, sees who He created us to be. He sees us through eyes of love that help move us toward the identity and purpose He has for us. He is not limited by merely what we are now.

His desire is that we would grow in our relationship with Him, and that we would share with others about His love for them and desire for them live in His design as well.

God is for us!

If you made that decision, talk with you Hope Unshakeable leader or email us at *info@hopefamilycare.net* for next steps on how to walk in true hope.

FEELINGS WHEEL

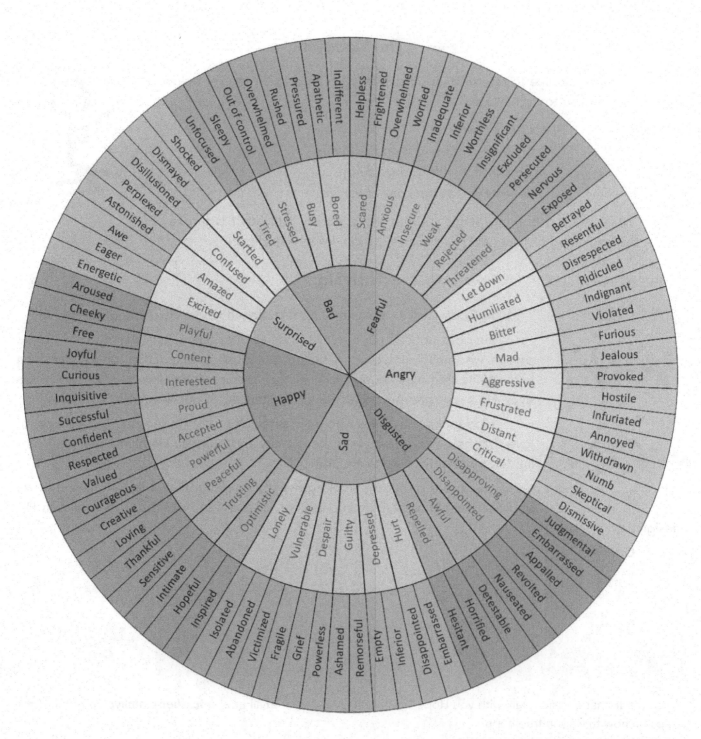

Credit: Geoffrey Roberts (Kaleen, Australia)

THANK YOU

We want to thank you for journeying through this time with us and the other grandparents in your group. Traveling a grief journey can be difficult and long, but it does not have to be traveled alone. By committing to do each of the weekly readings, showing up to the group, and sharing from your heart, you are moving forward!

If this small group study has been beneficial or encouraging to you. Please email us at *info@hopefamilycare.net* and share what God has done through this time. We would love to share your story as an encouragement to others.

Lastly, we would love to equip you to lead your own Hope Unshakeable Group. If that is your desire, please email us at info@hopefamilycare.net. We would love to have you join our team.

Our prayer for you is that you will find, in the group you have just journeyed with, people that you can call or text when you need that extra support. You will need them from time to time, but they will also need you. As you journey forward, do so together.

Together Hope Happens

Jeff and Mackenzie

Hope Family Care

Hope Family Care (HFC) is a nonprofit ministry that walks with families who have experienced the death of a child. They provide support and community for the whole family (parents, siblings, and grandparents) as they navigate their grief journey.

Support Offered:

- **Personal Support:** HFC reaches out to families who have experienced the loss of a child. The goal is to provide a safe place for families to be able to process their grief.

- **Hope Bags:** Hope Bags are filled with items that other child loss families have found helpful in the aftermath of their loss. They are free of charge, but donations are helpful to offset the cost of filling and sending them. You can send or request a Hope Bag at **www.HopeFamilyCare.net** by clicking on the **Hope Bags** tab under the **Hope** menu.

- **Hope Family Retreats:** Hope Family Retreats are held periodically throughout the year in various locations around the United States. They are for the entire family. While parents are meeting, older and younger siblings are working with sibling grief coordinators through age appropriate content that has been developed with the help of child therapists and counselors. Each sibling grief coordinator has lost a sibling; they understand the pain that the siblings experience when losing a brother or sister.

- **Community Groups:** HFC's desire is to connect families with communities either online or in person. These communities are based on this workbook or other studies that will help the families continue to walk forward on their grief journey.

- **Remembrance Events:** Remembering the children that have passed before us is important. HFC hosts or partners with remembrance events around the country at various times throughout the year. The two main times are in October for child loss awareness day and in December right before Christmas. These events, among others, help bring families together to remember the children they have lost, but also to connect them with others who understand the grief journey they are on.

- **Equipping Churches:** Supporting child loss families can be challenging for a church, especially if there is no one on staff who has that experience. HFC comes alongside churches to help equip them in practical, helpful ways to support child loss families. The goal is that these churches would become centers of hope in their communities for all families who experience the death of a child.

- **Resources Online:** There is a list of helpful resources that HFC has created online. To access the list of resources, visit **www.HopeFamilyCare.net** click on the **Resources** tab under the **Hope** menu.

Hope Family Care is here to support you on your grief journey. If you would like more information or support, please contact us via one of the ways below.

Connect with Hope Family Care:

Online:	HopeFamilyCare.net
Facebook:	@HopeFamilyCareMinistries
Instagram:	@HopeFamilyCareMinistries
Email:	info@HopeFamilyCare.net

ABOUT THE AUTHORS

Jeff and Mackenzie Rollins, who experienced the loss of their daughter Zoe, are the founders and visionaries behind the Hope Unshakeable Series, and Hope Family Care, a nonprofit organization that brings hope and healing to families who have experienced the death of a child. Through the sending of Hope Bags, Hope Family Retreats, and online and local groups, Hope Family Care has walked with hundreds of families across the US, Canada, and Latin America.

All of their married lives, the Rollins's have been ministering together. They have had the privilege of being youth leaders, ministering to students in the various schools where they have taught, as missionaries in Ecuador, through lay counseling, training and teaching on discipleship, and now as the founders of Hope Family Care.

Jeff and Mackenzie live just north of Houston, Texas, with three of their children, with great anticipation of being reunited with their daughter in Heaven one day soon.